For more than 30 years Alfred Malabre has interpreted economic news for over 6 million readers of *The Wall Street Journal*. As the *Journal's* economic news editor and featured columnist, Malabre has shared his insights into the "real world" of economics. Now, in *Understanding the New Economy*, he gives you a lively and highly readable primer on how today's economy works ... and how you can better assess and understand daily news reports.

Drawing on both his experience and his contacts with the top ranks of government and business, Malabre reveals the forces that drive our economy and explains:

- business cycles and why they occur

- the linkage between the economy and the stock market ... and how to benefit from it

- whether recessions are inevitable

- why economic forecasts should be taken with a grain of salt

- the United States in a global economy

- how to understand the "headline-grabbers"

This book offers you clear writing and keen insights into the nature of our economy. It is unburdened by the complex graphs, tables, and charts that are the staple of the economics classroom and the bane of readers and students.

Understanding the New Economy familiarizes you with the economic data you need to make an intelligent appraisal of where the economy stands today and where it may move in future weeks and months.

Understanding the New Economy

Understanding the New Economy

Alfred L. Malabre, Jr.
News Editor
The Wall Street Journal

Dow Jones-Irwin
Homewood, Illinois 60430

Dow Jones-Irwin is a trademark of Dow Jones & Company, Inc.

This publication is designed to provide accurate and authoritative information in regard to the subject matter covered. It is sold with the understanding that neither the author nor the publisher is engaged in rendering legal, accounting, or other professional service. If legal advice or other expert assistance is required, the services of a competent professional person should be sought.

From a Declaration of Principles jointly adopted by a Committee of the American Bar Association and a Committee of Publishers.

Sponsoring editor: Richard A. Luecke
Project editor: Jean Roberts
Production manager: Carma W. Fazio
Production services: Chernow Editorial Services
Jacket Design: STUDIO M
Compositor: Compset, Inc.
Typeface: 11/13 Century Schoolbook
Printer: Arcata Graphics/Kingsport

LIBRARY OF CONGRESS
Library of Congress Cataloging-in-Publication Data

Malabre, Alfred L.
    Understanding the new economy / Alfred L. Malabre, Jr.
      p.   cm.
    Includes index.
    ISBN 1-556-23117-2
    1. Economics. 2. United States—Economic conditions—1945–
I. Title.
HB171.M323 1989
330.973′092—dc19

88–15529
CIP

Printed in the United States of America

2 3 4 5 6 7 8 9 0 K 5 4 3 2 1 0 9 8

*Rededicated to
Mary Patricia, with gratitude for your
support and patience*

OTHER BOOKS BY MR. MALABRE

America's Dilemma: Jobs vs. Prices
Investing For Profit In The Eighties
Beyond Our Means

NOTE TO READERS

Back in 1975 I wrote a book entitled *Understanding the Economy: For People Who Can't Stand Economics*. It sold well. A lot of people either wanted to understand the economy or couldn't stand economics—I don't know which. This book is a direct descendant of that earlier work.

Many aspects of economic life have changed in the intervening 13 years. Much is truly "new," and I've tried to reflect that in the pages that follow. So much has changed that this is, in large part, a new book, not a revision. If you read the old book, we both know, for starters, that you're a lot older now. I hope that you'll enjoy reading this one.

CONTENTS

CHAPTER 1

SOME WORDS OF EXPLANATION

This book is for the person who wishes to keep reasonably well-informed about economic developments. It is for the interested layman who wants to gain a little perspective on the economic headlines that come at us daily from television, radio, and the newspapers. It is for the concerned *non*expert who seeks not expertise but enough familiarity with economic data to allow an intelligent personal appraisal of where the economy stands and where it may move in future weeks and months.

This is *not* a book for anyone wishing to study the social science of economics. It is *not* a book espousing any particular economic theory. It is *not* a book for anyone who is content merely to accept what others, in high or low positions, may be saying about the economy.

Most decidedly, this is *not* a textbook. Most decidedly, it urges no political point of view. The only converts it seeks are converts to a more enlightened assimilation of daily economic headlines.

Within these pages, you will find not a single formula or chart or graph. Nor will you encounter at the end any glossary of economic definitions. When you come to a term that requires defining, it will be defined on the spot.

At the end you will find an index. If you want to discover quickly what the gross national product is really all about, you can look it up in the index and then flip to the appropriate pages. You will obtain, I submit, a more useful description of what the GNP actually represents than could be provided by the standard glossary-type definition that appears in textbooks.

Just as this is by no stretch of the imagination an economics textbook, I am by no stretch of the imagination a professional economist. I am a newspaperman, employed by *The Wall Street Journal*. I happen to find considerable fascination in observing and writing about the American economy. But I would be hard-pressed to explain to you the difference between a regression series and a diffusion index. And I question whether you would care to have me explain. It would be a boring business.

There is nothing boring, however, about trying to understand some basic things about the nation's economy—what goes into it, what comes out of it, how we measure it, how it moves and changes, how it is influenced by the behavior of businessmen and the decisions, for better or for worse, of government officials and political leaders.

A fundamental premise of this book is that many Americans share an interest in such matters. But another premise is that an unfortunate combination of circumstances works to discourage people from becoming better informed about the economy. Almost without exception, the few good economic textbooks available are fat and forbidding, and they generally fail to provide such elementary information as where to find and how to read basic understandable gauges of the state of the country's economy.

The unhappy result is a dearth of fundamental material for the individual—student or interested layman—who merely wants to be able to regard the economic scene with a little common sense and sophistication.

"Economics as a science is not 'dismal'—as Thomas Carlyle once called it," says Charls E. Walker, a professional economist who served as a high official in the Treasury Department from 1969 to 1973. "The problem is that it has been dismally taught—if taught at all."

Speaking of the need for a greater understanding of the economy by the electorate, Mr. Walker remarks: "It is not a job that will be over soon, but we must get on with it or wake up some day to find ourselves with an economic system that nobody wants—one that performs poorly and fails to deliver in a manner that the people of the U.S. have come to expect. If our economic system does fail, the underpinnings of our participatory democracy will indeed be weakened and the chances of fulfilling the American dream will be greatly reduced."

Tilford Gaines, senior vice-president and economist of Manufacturers Hanover Trust Company, a large New York bank, once wrote: "It is amazing how ignorant most Americans are about the free-enterprise economic system and, particularly at the present moment, how little faith there is in its continued functioning. All educated people understand our political system and the checks and balances that have enabled it to work. All religious people understand the tenets of their faith. Each artisan or professional understands the rules of his trade. But how many understand the logical structures of our economy and importance of our economic institutions within our total social fabric?"

A survey has found that only about half of the nation's 60,000 social-studies teachers—those most likely to be teaching economics courses in schools—have had any formal training in economics. Another finding of the survey was that only about a quarter of the nation's junior-high-school students understand the difference between a free-enterprise economy and one that is completely government controlled.

What percentage of those students would be able to identify the Federal Open Market Committee and the fundamental role that committee plays in shaping America's economic future? My guess would be, at the most, a minuscule fraction of the 25 percent who managed to identify free enterprise.

As Charls Walker suggests, the way in which basic economics is generally taught may be to blame for much of the aversion to economic matters. Too frequently, introductory courses that should simply equip students with basic tools for understanding economic developments focus instead on boring, impractical theoretical matters. That may be fine for anyone moving on with economics as the major course of study. But it is of no discernible use to the student who merely wants to be able to digest the abundant economic news and perhaps make a few intelligent judgments.

A case in point is my own classroom experience with economics at Yale University shortly after World War II. Unfortunately, the classroom scene has not changed appreciably since then. The course at Yale, Econ 10, was a half-year affair, supposedly a simple introduction designed for students majoring in other fields. (Mine happened to be English.) The course consisted mainly of discussing assorted formulas and curves, drawn majestically on the classroom blackboard by the instructor. It was uninteresting in all respects; it had, so far as I could determine, not the faintest connection with the real world beyond the New Haven campus.

Benumbed and benighted, I managed—barely—to pass the course. But it remains to this day the one and only economics course that I have ever suffered through.

The economy can probably never be made as interesting as a good Alfred Hitchcock thriller. However, there is no need for it to be made dismally dull. The economy can be an intensely interesting subject—to nonexperts as well as professional economists. Moreover, it can be followed, by those willing to try, without any real difficulty. To follow it requires no in-depth scholarly comprehension of the intricate workings of the economy. But it does require common sense and a passing familiarity with what has happened in the past. No more expertise is needed than in understanding the more rudimentary baseball statistics (nothing so complicated as slugging percentages) and knowing the difference between two percent and two percentage points.

Parenthetically: you may discover, as a dividend to a better understanding of the economy, that you will be able to invest your money more wisely. Certainly, my own economy-watching over the years has enabled me to venture out occasionally with my crystal ball. I do recall, for example, a column of mine that appeared December 8, 1969—a gloomy time on Wall Street. The widely watched Dow Jones industrial-stock average stood at 785.04, down sharply from about 970 in mid-May of 1969. The economy clearly seemed headed into a recession. Unemployment was moving steadily upward. Corporate profits were sliding in the opposite direction. It hardly seemed an appropriate moment for a cheery, lighthearted appraisal of stock-market prospects. Yet, that was precisely what I produced for the *Journal's* readers that Monday morning.

"What the stock market needs," I cheerily started out, "is a good recession; there's nothing like a business slump to perk up stock prices." The column went on to suggest, on the basis of various statistics, that a recession indeed appeared imminent and that, consequently, most stock prices appeared quite reasonable. The column went so far as to forecast that stock prices, though due for a "sustained . . . rebound" from the December 1969 level, would probably flounder around for several months before beginning a big climb.

The record book shows that a recession did begin about that time—the National Bureau of Economic Research, official arbiter in such matters, places the start in November 1969. The record further shows that stock prices, measured by the Dow Jones average, did flounder around until May of 1970 and then began a sustained rise, gradual at first, that brought the average to 840 by the end of 1970 and to more than 950 early the next year. Thus, my 1969 column, had its advice been taken, would have enabled an investor to pick up some 165 points on the Dow Jones index in less than 18 months.

No training in economics or finance was responsible for the accuracy of that forecast. Rather, a little common sense research into business history was all that was necessary—research that anyone with an ability to read the English language and a mild tolerance for a few uncomplicated statistics could have undertaken. Even a cursory glance at the appropriate figures shows that stock prices often are higher at the pit of a business recession than around the peak of a preceding expansion period. In many instances, the rise in stock prices during a recession has been dramatic.

Nicholas Von Hoffman, an exceedingly able and articulate syndicated newspaper columnist, once observed that "time was when nobody but economists and upper-echelon people in big business paid attention to economic statistics," but now "the media throw more and more of those numbers at us."

This book will enable you to understand a lot more about what is coming at you the next time an announcer or a politician or a newspaper reporter starts spouting economic statistics. A particular figure on a particular day may be important, or it may not be. In any event—most importantly—you will be able to make that judgment for yourself.

CHAPTER 2

INTO THE 1990s

As we head into the 1990s and, beyond them, toward a new century, the matter of trying to understand, in fundamental terms, what America's economy is really all about assumes a fresh importance. Much has changed on the economic front since I wrote an earlier version of this book in 1975. In the intervening years, the economy has expanded sharply and endured severe downturns, the stock market has set new highs and taken record-shattering tumbles, and America's role on the world stage has diminished with the startling rise not only of Japan but of such formerly undeveloped nations as South Korea and Taiwan.

On a planet shrunken by new technology—for instance, in the areas of transportation and communications—it grows ever more apparent that swift change and global competition are the order of the day. It becomes imperative, in such an environment, to appreciate how our economy works, its underpinnings. If the stock market crashes, how does that relate to what economists call the business cycle? If overall economic activity expands strongly, how is that likely to affect the consumer price level?

With the many difficulties that have beset our economy in the more recent decades of the post–World War II era, it has become an easy matter, even fashionable, to take a cynical view of trying to make sense out of the economic scene, or out of what economists themselves are saying. The list of jokes about the profession, all unflattering, expands apace. For instance: Sound advice for economic forecasters is, If you give a number, don't give a date, or if you give a date, don't give a number, and if you're determined to keep forecasting, do it frequently. Or: Economists show that they have a sense of humor by their use of decimal points in their projections. Or: The length of an economic research report is inversely proportional to how well the economists producing it know what they're doing. Or: The more closely you look at the raw data in any economic analysis, the bigger trouble you're in. Or: An economist is someone who is good with numbers, like an accountant, but lacks the personality to be an accountant.

The list goes on, and grows even less charitable. And, though it clearly smacks of high hyperbole, it does reflect a deepening dismay over a seeming inability among the people expected to do so to assess the nation's economic performance in convincing fashion and provide sound advice for policy makers.

Indeed, there has developed a widespread sense that, in economic policy-making at least, we have entered a sort of Euripidean era, to recall a dismal progression in ancient Greek playwriting. In the plays of Aeschylus, in the early period, the particular tragic hero inevitably suffers but learns from this and emerges a better person, blessed with a new, heightened awareness. In the plays of Sophocles, in the middle Greek phase, the hero once again suffers but learns little from this. However, some benefit is derived because others, such as the audience, do gain valuable insight. In Euripides, in the final phase, the suffering continues, but it is pointless, with no discernible good coming out of it. All is senseless and cynicism prevails.

Something like this disheartening transformation has occurred over the last several decades on the economic front. In the early postwar years, there was a general sense among government and business leaders in the United States that, while America's economy was hardly immune to trouble, it could be made to expand smoothly and continuously with the proper mix of fiscal policies. Indeed, in the middle 1960s, during Lyndon Johnson's presidency, something akin to what the Greeks called *hubris*—overweening pride—set in in policy-making circles, so that eminent economists, who should have known better, became convinced that a sort of perpetual prosperity was in prospect. What the future held instead, it developed, was what the Greek playwrights deemed the ultimate stage in the tragic progression, inevitably following on the heels of *hubris*. They called it *ate*—devastation, despair, defeat. Or, in terms of the postwar

American economy, spiraling inflation, wrenching downswings in economic activity, periodic double-digit jobless levels reminiscent of the 1930s, and Brobdingnagian deficits in both the federal budget and foreign trade.

With such difficulties, it is no surprise that a sort of Euripidean cynicism tended to take hold. Reenforcing the disillusionment has been the inability of successive schools of economic thought to set things right. In the Johnson presidency, the assumption was that economic prosperity could be assured, in the main, through adroit manipulation of taxes and federal spending, a prescription based largely on the writings of John Maynard Keynes, the British economist. Relatively little heed was paid to monetary policy, what was happening to the nation's supply of money, under regulation by the Federal Reserve Board. A decade or so—and a severe recession—later, during Jimmy Carter's White House tenure, there was a shift to the so-called monetarist approach to economic management, which tied the growth of the money supply to the economy's own estimated capacity to expand. The hope, once again unfounded, was that monetarism would lead to uninterrupted economic gains, turning slumps, inflation, and the like into nothing more than distant, unpleasant memories. The chief advocate of this shift to monetarism was a Nobel-laureate economist from the University of Chicago. Milton Friedman, of whom we shall hear more later.

After monetarism came the so-called supply-side economists, led by Arthur Laffer, a fast-talking, publicity-loving California-based professor who managed to convince Ronald Reagan, among others, that the path to sustained prosperity was through neither Keynes nor Friedman but something he called the Laffer curve, a parabola which he first transcribed for an inquiring journalist on a cocktail napkin in a Washington, D.C., bar. The essence of the supply-side notion was that tax rates were far too high, discouraging productivity and saving. Moreover, the Laffer school held that rate reductions would unleash such a burst of economic activity that the federal budget balance would actually tend to strengthen, rather than sink ever more deeply into the red on account of diminished tax revenues.

Of course, the budget did sink into much deeper deficit after the supply-side tax cuts were enacted early in the Reagan presidency. At the same time, productivity continued to stagnate in most businesses, and savings, in terms of income, reached the lowest readings since the Great Depression.

The inability of any particular school of economic thought to produce a recession-proof, inflation-proof strategy should not be taken as a reason to despair of trying to gain a fuller understanding of how our economy works. Indeed, the failure in recent decades of so many different policy-making schools to produce the desired economic results is all the more reason for us to try to see where the difficulties may lie, to try to understand the economy's limits, as well as its potential. If for no other reason—and there are many—such an understanding is crucial when political office seekers proclaim from the soapbox, as they are wont to do, their wonder-prescriptions for economic salvation.

You will find no such remedies on these pages. But neither will you come away sensing that nothing can work, that any serious effort to achieve a sounder economic performance inevitably must fail. On the contrary, we will see that our economy has made great strides in the postwar decades and is surely capable of much further progress—but this inescapably will entail difficulty, for that is how the economy advances, never in a straight, uninterrupted line up, never without the occasional slump, never enjoying the sort of recessionless prosperity advertised by the ever squabbling proponents of this or that or the other school of economic thought.

If there is a judgment to be made here, it is that the economy can indeed be managed, made to work, but not through any quick fixes, not through simply pushing the right monetarist or fiscalist or supply-side button. As a wise physician once told me, everything should be done in moderation, and that applies as well to economic policy-making as to health. And, in a nation as free as ours, where so much depends on enlightenment at the ballot box, it becomes extra crucial that this be understood. If this book generates a healthy skepticism about economic panaceas, that is fine. It should not, however, lead anyone to cynicism.

A skeptical, realistic—but never cynical or despairing—assessment of the American business scene as the century winds down suggests, ultimately, that our economy is both "new" and "old." It is new in the sense that we have learned most painfully in recent decades that prosperity no longer will come as easily as, say, in the early postwar years, when much of the developed world, but not America, was disrupted by global conflict. And the economy is old in the sense that the same fundamentals and intertwined relationships that pertained 30 or 40 years ago, as well as earlier, continue to do so—to cite an illustration, within the framework of the business cycle, the roles played by money growth and spending, by profits and prices, by productivity and saving.

Precisely because the going has recently grown tougher, these basics demand far closer scrutiny and better understanding now than decades ago, when times, at least on the economic front, seemed easier and simpler. If we are able to appreciate, for instance, exactly how the Federal Reserve Board undertakes to regulate the growth of money and the level of interest rates, if we can grasp what the term "money" actually encompasses, then we are better able to render a sound judgment the next time a campaigning politician calls for the Fed, say, to bring down interest rates posthaste or to open a monetary spigot that may already be open wide.

It is only possible, in sum, to understand the new economy by understanding the old one. They are the same. The fundamentals that applied yesterday continue to apply today and also will do so tomorrow.

CHAPTER 3

THE HEADLINE GRABBERS

Just what do we mean when we talk about "the economy"?

We often say that the economy "looks good" or the economy "looks bad." What do we mean? What is the economy, really, and how can we keep a tab on it?

There are countless ways of looking at the economy. It encompasses an infinitely diverse range of business activity that transpires daily in the nation. A man drives from his home to his office in the morning. Along the way, he stops to buy a newspaper. At the office, he goes to the cafeteria and purchases a cup of coffee. Back at his desk, he picks up the phone and places a long-distance call to an associate in a city 2,000 miles away.

As far as the man is concerned, only the phone call is directly a part of his business endeavors. But in the larger picture—as far as the overall U.S. economy is concerned—every one of his actions contributes to the nation's general level of economic activity. The drive to the office, buying the newspaper, the coffee, and the telephone call all tend to expand overall economic activity. All are a part—albeit a minuscule fraction—of what we really are talking about when we mention "the economy."

To go from such tiny segments of the nation's economic scene to surveying the entire economy with reasonable intelligence requires a familiarity with some basic statistics compiled largely by highly trained analysts in various branches of the federal government, particularly in the Commerce Department, the Labor Department, the Federal Reserve Board, and the Treasury Department. Each of these government divisions issues wide-ranging data that help give us, if we merely know where to look and how to look, a better grasp of the overall economic picture.

PEOPLE

There is an old saw that defines the difference between a recession and a depression thus: *A recession is when your neighbor is unemployed and a depression is when you are unemployed.*

A better way to see whether the economy is in a recession or depression, or neither, is to take a look at the nation's overall unemployment rate. This is issued on a monthly basis by the Labor Department's Bureau of Labor Statistics in Washington. The BLS also provides monthly reports on the level of unemployment within various categories of the labor force—adult men, adult women, teenagers, married men, blacks and other minority races, whites, white-collar workers, blue-collar workers, nonagricultural workers, construction workers, workers who manufacture such "durable" goods as automobiles and appliances, and so on and so on.

A glance at the BLS report will show whether 4 percent, 6 percent, 8 percent, 10 percent, or whatever portion of the labor force is unemployed during a given month—that is, wants work but can't find work. The BLS report even carries the unemployment rate out to one decimal point for all the categories. The report also shows the trend of joblessness: whether the latest month's rate is higher or lower, for example, than a month earlier or a year earlier. It also provides absolute figures for the various worker categories, along with the percentages.

It's possible, in a given month, for instance, to have the unemployment rate rise at the same time that the number of jobholders in the country rises. The explanation can simply be that the number of persons entering the labor force and seeking work rose more sharply than usual in the particular month. This is precisely what happened, for example, between August and September of 1974. In that period, the overall unemployment rate jumped from 5.4 percent of the labor force to 5.8 percent. At first glance, the rise in joblessness suggests a deterioration in the country's labor situation. However, a closer inspection of BLS figures turns up the fact—not mentioned in the black headlines of rising unemployment—that employment also climbed substantially during the period, from 86,187,000 to 86,538,000—a rise in jobholders of about 350,000 in a single month. A further perusal of BLS statistics for the period provides a clear explanation of the paradox. The percentage of the country's working-age population employed or seeking work climbed from 61.7 percent in August to 62.1 percent in September. That percentage rise may seem insignificantly small, but it translates into a rise in the country's total labor force of nearly 800,000 persons. A major factor, of course, is the rising number of American women who wish to work.

In sum, a close look at all the job statistics, not just the overall unemployment rate, shows that the economy actually provided substantially more jobs during the period. However, the increase was not swift enough to accommodate the sharp rise in persons seeking work.

The lesson, clearly, for anyone wishing to gain a reasonable perspective on this important facet of economic activity, is that it pays to inspect more than simply the raw BLS figure for the overall unemployment rate.

Yet, unhappily, it is this raw figure that always seems to grab the headlines, even in newspapers that should know better and that try to provide their readers with a balanced picture of the country's actual labor situation. In the end, all too often, it is the raw figure that stirs passions in Congress and on Main Street, and ultimately provokes legislative and other action in Washington that again and again in the recent past has led to overstimulation of business in well-intentioned but questionable efforts to reduce unemployment.

An illustration of this tendency occurred early in 1975. In figures released by the BLS in early February, the overall unemployment rate took a particularly sharp jump, to 8.2 percent of the labor force in January from 7.2 percent in December. The headlines were even bigger and blacker than usual. The Ford administration, which until then had seemed reluctant to adopt economic policies that might possibly risk a revival of severe inflation in the country, came under sharp attack from all sorts of opinion leaders. George Meany, at the time the president of the powerful A.F.L–C.I.O., expressed outrage that President Ford was not taking drastic action to curb the climbing joblessness.

Within less than a week, as the criticism from Mr. Meany and others continued to mount, President Ford began to alter his previous cautious economic stance. On February 11, for example, only four days after the BLS report of 8.2 percent unemployment, the President dramatically announced that he would release some $2 billion of impounded highway construction funds to help create jobs.

The President's abrupt decision shows how a single economic statistic can command the headlines and, if it generates enough public clamor, can directly alter the course of Washington policy, and ultimately the course of the economy and, possibly, the nation. The wisdom of Mr. Ford's decision, of course, could be challenged on the ground that it encouraged highway building at a time when the nation was attempting, not very successfully, to conserve fuel. But it could also be challenged for another reason, one that could be perceived only by persons willing to read well beyond the black headlines of 8.2 percent unemployment. The details of the January job figures showed that the unemployment rate for heads of households, the family breadwinners, rose only to 5.2 percent from 4.6 percent in December. The rate for married men rose only to 4.5 percent from 3.8 percent. And the so-called hardship unemployment rate, people out of work 15 weeks or more, inched up to 1.7 percent from 1.4 percent. Unemployment among persons out of work 27 weeks or more held at less than 1 percent—to be exact, 0.7 percent—hardly the sort of level that Mr. Meany's outraged cries would lead one to anticipate.

Remarking on such little-noticed statistics, Albert H. Cox Jr., former chief economist of Lionel D. Edie & Co., a New York investment research concern owned by Merrill Lynch, Pierce, Fenner & Smith, Inc., the world's largest stock-brokerage house, wrote at the time: "News media and politicians are continuing to exaggerate and distort the issue of unemployment. With the release of last month's estimated total unemployment rate of 8.2 percent, headlines created visions of the Great Depression and all its extreme hardships. The facts . . . clearly contradict such impressions, but the illusion is leading both the Administration and Congress to over-react by spending too much money, a significant portion of which will not be covered by taxation. . . . This raises the threat of another boom-bust cycle."

On the same day that Mr. Cox made his comments, a short news item appeared in *The Wall Street Journal*. It carried no large headlines and received scant attention. It reported that "low-status jobs remain hard to fill, despite surging unemployment." One "key reason for the situation," the *Journal* article stated, appeared to be that many of the jobless were able to get along adequately on unemployment insurance, food stamps, and welfare. The article went on to report, for example, that a Chicago taxi company found that applications for hard-to-fill cabbie jobs declined whenever "President Ford announced new unemployment benefits." Also noting this phenomenon, Lionel Edie's Mr. Cox declared that "unemployment and welfare benefits have now risen to the point where they create unemployment."

At this point, it may be worth inserting a few parenthetical words about just how the BLS obtains its unemployment statistics. Briefly, pollsters hired by the Census Bureau, a branch of the Commerce Department, each month canvass many thousands of households scattered across the nation.

Julius Shiskin, as commissioner of the BLS, once explained how this process works. The pollsters, mostly women working part-time, go to these households and ask various questions. After the initial interview, follow-up interviews are conducted by telephone, with follow-up questions that help determine such matters as degree of hardship, duration of unemployment, and so on.

"If I were given a large amount of extra money, I would get more details on unemployment in local areas," Mr. Shiskin told an interviewer from *U.S. News & World Report*. "Today, the unemployment figures are being used for allocating billions of dollars' worth of manpower revenue funds—federal money going out to localities to be used for manpower training and public-service jobs. Still, we are having to estimate local-area unemployment all over the country on the basis of a 47,000-household national sample. We recently got money to add some 13,000 households to our monthly survey, and that will eventually give us better data."

A sample question from the pollsters: "Is anyone here looking for a job?" The BLS counts as unemployed anyone who is not employed and has actively looked for a job in the preceding four weeks but hasn't managed to land one.

This procedure leads to including among the jobless such

persons as, for example, a housewife who may be looking for a job between 1 P.M. and 4 P.M. on weekdays, or a college student seeking work for two weeks during his Christmas vacation.

At the other end of the spectrum, I should add, are the so-called discouraged unemployed, who have given up job-hunting and, when surveyed by the Census Bureau people, may answer that no, they haven't been job-seeking during the last four weeks. These unfortunate individuals, numbering more than a million in 1975, according to rough BLS estimates, are not included in the official, overall unemployment figures. The category unquestionably does include thousands of helpless cases. However, BLS analysts estimate, it also includes countless individuals who have become "discouraged" from job hunting simply because, for example, they can't find work that they deem commensurate with their inflated ideas of their own abilities. It is lamentable that no governmental agency compiles and issues any statistical index that shows the number of job vacancies in the country. Preliminary work toward such an index was undertaken in the early 1970s. But the project was abandoned. Some observers say it was dropped more for political reasons—to assuage minority groups and Congressional liberals—than for any technical difficulties in compiling such a yardstick.

The survey technique of the BLS has obvious advantages. It seeks to ensure that our unemployment statistics don't overlook most persons who really are jobless. But another result, many analysts believe, is that on balance it tends to inflate U.S. unemployment levels, particularly when they are compared, as they often are, to those in other major industrial countries.

In Britain, for example, unemployment rates are based on the actual number of persons who take the trouble to go to government facilities and register themselves as being out of work and wanting a job. It has been estimated that British unemployment rates, if they were calculated using the U.S. method, would be appreciably higher than they are stated to be in the official British reports.

In the United States, unemployment among black teenagers is carefully calculated each month. The jobless rate for this age-race category in some years has crossed above the horrendous 40 percent level. A factor in high teenage joblessness, especially among blacks, is that the United States has on the books a minimum-wage statute that applies to teenagers as well as older workers. Recently, some U.S. officials tried to extract from Congress a change in minimum-wage regulations that would have allowed slightly lower minimums for teenage workers than for adults. The proposal has been bitterly opposed by organized labor in the United States, particularly by the powerful A.F.L.–C.I.O. Apparently the labor chieftains fear that their breadwinner members, their prime constituents, might ultimately lose some jobs to lesser-paid teenage competition.

It cannot be proved beyond a doubt that the inclusion of teenagers among those fully covered by minimum-wage regulations is the major reason that teenage joblessness runs so high in the United States. But there certainly may be a good deal more than a slight connection. Anyone who has had to engage a teenager for an odd summer job knows the problems involved. All too often, you end up mowing the lawn yourself.

How many American teenagers today spend their summers in idleness, possibly developing bad habits and getting into trouble with their families and even the law, simply because there is little or no gainful employment available for them at the minimum wage?

The situation abroad is another thing, obviously, to keep in mind when you next ponder a gloomy headline about high teenage unemployment in the United States.

Altogether, we can see from this look behind and around the U.S. unemployment headlines that the state of the economy—recession, depression, or neither—involves far more than simply who happens to be unemployed—you, your child, your neighbor, or the fellow down the street. The big picture can indeed be glimpsed—but this must be done with much caution and in the fullest possible perspective. The necessary statistics, most of them turned out monthly by the BLS, are there for those willing to take a little time to look.

As a very rough rule of thumb, some economists draw the line between a recession and a depression by whether the overall unemployment rate is less than a double-digit figure. If unemployment comes to 9 percent of the labor force, some analysts would say, the economy is only in a recession. But if it reaches or exceeds the 10 percent mark, they would place the economy in a state of depression. To put the matter in perspective: Unemployment reached about 25 percent of the labor force during the pit of the Great Depression of the 1930s, and the rate remained in double digits until World War II was under way for the United States. Using double-digit unemployment as a yardstick of economic health, the Great Depression ran throughout the entire decade of the 1930s, encompassing, as we shall see in a later chapter, two extensive periods of business "recovery" as well as two periods of severely contracting economic activity. Not until the pit of the 1981 to 1982 economic slump did the jobless rate, reaching 11 percent, again enter double-digit territory. Some economists label that slump depressionary, others recessionary.

PRODUCTS

The labor situation is often the first thing that pops into mind, and into the headlines, when questions arise about the health of the economy. This is doubly true if unemployment happens to strike close to home. But there are other ways of keeping a tab on the big economic picture. Another headline grabber—one that many economists scrutinize far more thoroughly than the unemployment figures—is the gross national product, or the GNP, a supposedly all-encompassing economic figure turned out by Washington's statistical mills. A simple and somewhat superficial definition of the GNP can be readily devised. It is nothing less than the estimated value in the marketplace of the country's total output of goods and services. To quote from a study by the Federal Reserve Bank of Philadelphia, entitled *The Mystery of Economic Growth,* when the GNP "goes up, most people think we are growing—the economy is producing more, they say." Paul A. Samuelson—the widely read professor of economics at Massachusetts Institute of Technology, Nobel prize–winner, and columnist on business matters—has called the GNP "one of the most important concepts in all economics" because it "measures the economic performance of the whole economy."

The GNP is "gross," all right. In 1988, it approximated $5

trillion. A trillion, in case you have forgotten or aren't familiar with such lofty numbers, is one with a dozen zeroes after it.

Unlike the unemployment rate, the GNP figure comes out only once a quarter and invariably has to be revised and revised and revised, sometimes over many years, as Washington statisticians strive to make their estimates of past economic activity levels more precise and accurate. GNP data is compiled and issued by the Commerce Department. Like the BLS, the Commerce Department is a primary government source for the broad-gauge sort of data that help us to grasp the overall condition of the economy. A close look at the Commerce Department figure makes it easy to understand why the GNP is generally regarded as the ultimate single measure of the total economic situation. Its components—the categories that made up the $5 trillion figure in 1988—include all major areas of business endeavor.

The vast scope of the GNP coverage can be indicated by reviewing in very general terms the major categories that Commerce Department analysts add together to arrive at an overall figure. The first and largest, accounting for nearly two thirds of the GNP, is a category embracing all consumer spending in the country. It, in turn, is divided into three subgroups: "durable" goods such as automobiles, appliances, and furniture; "nondurable" goods such as clothing, food, and fuel; and "services," such as home-maintenance and transportation expenses.

The second major GNP category covers nongovermental investment-type spending for everything from housing to machine tools to new factories to warehouse supplies. This category accounts for just over 15 percent of the GNP.

The third major GNP category takes into account all government outlays. This category, which is divided into federal defense spending, other federal spending, and expenditures by state and local governments, amounts to another 15 percent or so of the GNP.

The fourth category that makes up the GNP figure embraces U.S. exports and imports of goods and services. If the export total happens to exceed the import total at a particular time, the difference is added to the GNP figure; if not, the difference is subtracted.

Normally, this difference—called the country's balance of trade—is tiny in terms of the other major GNP categories. As we will discover later, however, the balance of trade carries a significance that far exceeds its apparently minor importance in the GNP statistics.

If we may return momentarily to our friend going to work, we can see where his various activities fit into the makeup of the GNP. His purchase of the car that he drives to work shows up in the durable goods subgroup of the consumer-spending category. The gasoline consumed on the way to work is in the same major category but under the nondurable subgroup. So are the newspapers and the cup of coffee. The cost of the long-distance telephone call comes under the services subgroup. The cost of buying business equipment in his office falls into the large category that includes nongovernmental spending. If our man happened to be working for, say, the Commerce Department instead of a private concern, the equipment would show up under the large GNP category covering government outlays, in the subgroup for expenditures for other than defense purposes.

Just as unemployment figures have to be viewed with caution, so do GNP statistics—but for very different reasons. Unemployment figures, of course, involve numbers of people. But GNP data, as we have already seen, are expressed in terms of American dollars. And American dollars, unlike American people, have shrunk rather drastically over the years since World War II—on account of inflation. The upshot is that GNP statistics can provide a very misleading view of the overall economy if they are not somehow adjusted to allow for inflation. For instance, 1974 is conceded to have been a year of sharply contracting business activity in the United States. Yet the country's GNP actually rose by nearly $100 billion during the year.

That hardly sounds like an economy in trouble. The trouble shows up when the figures are adjusted for rising prices. The adjusted GNP figure that results is, appropriately, called the "real" GNP, and it certainly seems to be a good deal more realistic than the unadjusted GNP figure, at least in inflationary times.

Let us take another look at the 1974 record, using the real

GNP as the yardstick. This economic yardstick actually declined on the order of $40 billion during the year—a far cry from the huge increase of $100 billion registered by the unadjusted GNP figure.

The adjustment process used by Commerce Department statisticians is a complicated matter and will not be detailed here. Briefly, however, it can be stated that the statisticians attempt to adjust for inflation throughout the economy, at all levels of transaction; not just, say, at the consumer price level, where you or I might enter the picture when we buy food at the supermarket or clothing or appliances at the store.

As a result of such efforts, the real GNP unquestionably provides a much clearer picture of the general economic health of the nation than the unadjusted figure. But even the real GNP has its drawbacks and should not be taken unquestioningly as the ultimate measure of where the economy stands.

The validity of the real GNP—as well as of the unadjusted GNP figure from which it is largely derived—hinges on the accuracy of the diverse statistics that it comprises. The GNP concept is so all-inclusive that it is also, unavoidably, vulnerable to large miscalculations and downright errors in the course of its compilation.

Oskar Morgenstern, a noted economics professor who conducted highly critical analyses of GNP data over the years, may have overstated the case only slightly when he once told an audience at New York University: "Alas, the GNP concept is primitive in the extreme." Many of his complaints about the statistic cannot be denied. He correctly noted, for example, that "many services are rendered and many goods are produced that never enter a market" and therefore never show up anywhere in any of the categories or subsections of the GNP.

A delightful absurdity in the GNP concept, remarked upon by Dr. Morgenstern and others, is that the household duties performed by housewives—cooking, cleaning, and the like—are nowhere considered in GNP data. Yet if the same duties are performed by a hired maid, the services subsection of consumer spending accordingly increases, giving a small feminine boost to the overall economy—at least as it is represented by the GNP measures, real or unadjusted for price changes. It is not entirely facetious to contend that the economy, as described by GNP or real GNP statistics, would tend to expand appreciably faster than it has done in recent years if every wife in the country simply hired herself out as a maid to work for the family next door.

Another problem with the GNP concept, as Dr. Morgenstern and other analysts have observed, is that it records as positive contributions to overall economic activity events that really represent a malfunctioning of the economic system. Dr. Morgenstern used this illustration:

> If we are stuck in one of the thousands of traffic jams, if airplanes are stacked and cannot land on schedule, if fires break out and other disasters occur that require repair—up goes the GNP. More gasoline is used, fares go up, overtime has to be paid, and so on. It would be difficult in any other science [than economics] to find a measure which tells simultaneously opposite stories of the functioning of a complex system in one ... number. If we merely improve the scheduling of airplanes and stagger the times of automobile traffic, and nothing else is changed—down goes GNP. It goes up, on the other hand, if industry pollutes the air and we create other industries which remove the polluting substances.

PRICES

A third key feature of the overall economic scene that has managed in recent years to grab headlines with impressive regularity is the subject of inflation. Indeed, in the late 1960s and 1970s, it seems safe to say that no other facet of the economy— for good reason—attracted such attention. It also may be said, however, that keeping an accurate tab on inflation can be every bit as tricky as maintaining a clear view of the labor situation or the true position of the gross national product.

When people talk about "inflation" and when a newspaper headline proclaims PRICES CLIMB TO RECORD LEVEL, this refers normally to the latest consumer-price report of the BLS, the same government statistics mill that puts out the unemployment rate.

That aforementioned fellow who drives to work, buys a

newspaper and coffee, and makes a phone call from his office may read on the front page of his newspaper that inflation is getting worse. If his newspaper happens to cost him more than, say, the day before, he will have dramatic, firsthand evidence of worsening inflation. In any event, if he reads much beyond that inflation headline, the chances are he will find that the fine print of the article actually reports that the BLS index of consumer prices a month ago rose above its level in the preceding month.

Unfortunately, such articles seldom go into much detail about the movement of different items constituting the consumer-price index (or simply the CPI). But the BLS does in fact provide considerable detail with regard to individual items. In the monthly reports of the BLS, the CPI is broken down into three major categories—food, other commodities, and services. These categories, in turn, are broken down. The food category, for instance, shows monthly price trends for such diverse items as cereals, bakery products, meats, poultry, fish, dairy products, fruits, vegetables, and, in a special subsection, food eaten away from home. The category embracing all other commodities is split into three parts—all nondurable goods, nondurable goods other than clothing, and durable goods. Each of these parts is further divided into subsections covering such diverse items as gasoline, motor oil, tobacco products, alcoholic beverages, fuel oil, and coal. The third major CPI category, covering services, provides price information on rent, medical care, and transit fares, among others.

The BLS also provides monthly price information for different urban areas. At the same time that the bureau releases its overall consumer-price data for the nation as a whole each month, it reports in detail the consumer-price trend in Chicago, Detroit, the Los Angeles–Long Beach area, the New York–Northeastern New Jersey area, Philadelphia, Boston, Houston, Pittsburgh, Cleveland, Dallas, Washington, St. Louis, and the San Francisco–Oakland area.

The CPI is based on prices of approximately 400 items that BLS analysts have chosen to represent the movement of prices of all goods and services purchased by wage earners and clerical workers in urban areas—which by definition includes residents of towns with as few as 2,500 people. Prices for these items are collected by shoppers trained by the BLS. They buy at some 24,000 business establishments around the country, including grocery and department stores, hospitals, filling stations, and the like. Mailed questionnaires are also used by the bureau to keep track of price trends involving such items as local transit fares and public-utility rates. The CPI expresses its monthly index in terms of the average price level prevailing during 1967, the so-called base year for many economic indexes. The report that the CPI stood at 156.1 in January, 1975, for example, is another way of saying that consumer prices, on the average, rose 56.1 percent between 1967 and January 1975.

The relative importance assigned in the monthly index to individual items is based on a BLS study of the spending habits of some 10,000 families. A major criticism of the index is that such studies are conducted only once a decade, and occasionally not even that often. The criticism, clearly valid, holds that consumer spending habits change more frequently, and that unless these changes are monitored more often the CPI becomes increasingly misleading. BLS officials claim that a limited budget precludes more regular studies.

In any event, occasional updating does take place. In the mid-1970s, for instance, BLS analysts assigned an importance, or "weight," of about 25 percent to food, 39 percent to nonfood commodities, and 36 percent to services, within the overall CPI. This was a change from, say, 1970, when food's weight, for instance, was only 22 percent. In attempting to keep the index as realistic as possible, the BLS also made changes in items monitored. It started pricing, among other things, between-meal snacks, motel rooms, garbage disposal units, moving expenses, parking fees, taxi fares, outboard motors, golf fees, college tuition, music lessons, legal fees, and funeral charges. At the same time, items dropped from the list, on the theory that they now constitute too minor a part of consumer spending patterns, included lemons, nightgowns, pajamas, appendectomies, and sewing machines.

Other unpriced expenses included income taxes, personal property taxes, and Social Security taxes. Sales and real estate taxes, however, are regularly measured by BLS samplers.

The importance of the CPI, it should be noted, extends far

beyond simply providing us with a means of keeping track of inflation. Incomes of roughly half the U.S. population are linked, through so-called escalator clauses in labor contracts and other pay arrangements, to changes in the CPI.

The CPI is used as a so-called deflator of many other economic series, to adjust them for price changes from month to month, as well as to translate them into inflation-free—or constant as opposed to current—dollars. Examples include retail sales and hourly and weekly earnings. CPI components, moreover, are used as deflators for most personal consumption spending that goes into the calculation of the gross national product, the broadest available gauge of overall economic activity.

In addition, the CPI is employed to adjust all sorts of income payments. More than 8.5 million workers are covered by collective-bargaining contracts which provide for increases in wage rates based on increases in the index. Besides private-sector workers whose wages or pensions are adjusted according to changes in the CPI, the index also affects the earnings of more than 80 million persons, largely as a result of statutory action. These include some 40 million Social Security beneficiaries, some 4 million retired military and federal Civil Service employees and survivors, and about 20 million food stamp recipients. Changes in the CPI also affect some 23 million schoolchildren who eat lunch at school. Under the National School Lunch Act, national average payments for those lunches and breakfasts must be adjusted annually by the Secretary of Agriculture on the basis of the change in the CPI component called "food away from home." In addition, the National Recovery Act of 1981 provides for adjustments to the income tax structure based on the change in the CPI, so as to prevent inflation-caused creep into higher tax brackets.

A few words should perhaps be inserted here about the origins of the CPI. One of the oldest economic series, it was launched during World War I, when rapid increases in prices, especially in shipbuilding centers, made such an index essential for reckoning cost-of-living adjustments in shipyard pay. To provide a correct weighting formula for the index, studies of family spending patterns were subsequently made in 92 industrial centers during the period 1917 to 1919. Periodic collection of prices was begun, and the index was estimated back to 1913. The most recent major revision in expenditure weights was completed in 1987. It incorporated new weights, with increased importance assigned to such categories as entertainment, food away from home, apparel, and new vehicles, and less weight given to such spending areas as food at home, motor fuel, and medical care. In all, there are seven major expenditure groups—food and beverages, housing, apparel and upkeep, transportation, medical care, entertainment, and other goods and services—and these are subdivided into 69 so-called expenditure classes, which in turn are split into 184 specific item categories. These range from white bread to college tuition to women's suits.

The BLS also has constructed a second index, a more broadly based CPI for "all urban consumers"—dubbed the CPI-U—that takes into account the buying patterns of professional and salaried workers, part-time workers, the self-employed, the jobless, and retired people. The CPI-U supplements the so-called CPI-W, which covers only wage earners and clerical workers. The two indexes, however, continue to move in very similar fashion, with the CPI-U more commonly used by various prices watchers.

"An increase of only 1 percent in the index results in some $1 billion in additional wages and other payments to the American people," according to a study by Towers, Perrin, Forster & Crosby, a Philadelphia-based management-consulting firm. The report adds: "Because the cost of living and inflation have become the Siamese twins of modern-day economic discussion, it is vital to understand what the CPI is, what it is not, and what it should be."

In passing: A delightful, semiserious attempt to gauge cost-of-living trends for the well-to-do has been made by Raymond F. DeVoe, Jr., a stock broker well known along Wall Street for the whimsy that he manages to inject into matters economic. He has worked up something that he calls the "Cost of Living It Up Index," or simply the CLIUI. Mr. DeVoe's index, based on his own experiences in New York, as well as on reports from his wealthier cocktail-party acquaintances, covers price trends of such items as caviar, Pucci scarves, maids, private schools, mink coats, maintenance charges in large Park Avenue apartments, Brooks Brothers neckties, Countess Mara neckties, summer camps in Maine, annual tuition at Harvard, veterinarians' fees, silver baby cups at Tiffany, gold jewelry, a shoeshine with tip, employing a bartender at home, employing Jim Buck dog walkers, a ticket to see the New York Knicks, a ticket to see a Broadway musical, dinner at Le Mistral, a Beefeater martini, *The Monthly Labor Review,* a parlor-car ticket on the Cannonball train from New York to Southampton, and annual dues at the University Club.

In all, 72 items are included in Mr. DeVoe's CLIUI, which in one 12-month period in the 1970s soared about 20 percent, he estimates, or roughly twice as rapidly as the far less fascinating CPI climbed in the same 12 months.

The economic impact of relatively minor alterations in the CPI was pointed out vividly in a 1975 article in *Barron's,* a weekly business magazine, titled "Figures Do Lie." In December 1974, the article recalled, the BLS discovered that it had erred slightly in its monthly CPI report, so that the reported index was one tenth of a point higher than it should have been. That hardly sounds like a very significant miscalculation, but *Barron's* noted that if the error had been allowed to stand it would have meant, in the course of a year, an overpayment of a penny an hour to, among others, 10,000 employees of Kennecott Copper Corporation. It would have cost the company, many of whose employees are covered by the aforementioned escalator clauses in their labor contracts, more than $200,000.

Altogether, it's not in the least surprising that the CPI is the most widely followed measure of inflation. It is broad-ranging and readily comprehensible. But it is a fact that not all economists turn first to the CPI when they wish to ascertain the economy's overall price situation—broad as it is, the CPI is not the most comprehensive price yardstick available. That distinction belongs to a far less renowned inflation gauge, one that rarely makes the headlines. It is called, somewhat forbiddingly, the GNP price deflator.

Unlike the monthly CPI, the GNP deflator is issued only quarterly, and not by the BLS but by the Commerce Department. And despite its forbidding name, it is not really that complicated a statistic. Essentially, it is a measure of the difference between the GNP and the real GNP. It is obtained simply by dividing the GNP for a given period by the real GNP for the same period. When this division has been performed, it is possible to see whether the GNP deflator has been rising or falling and at what rate. It's worth noting that the movement of the deflator usually closely parallels the movement of the CPI but is rarely identical to it. In 1974, for example, the CPI rose about 11 percent and the deflator about 10 percent. One explanation for the difference is that the year's inflationary pressures were more heavily concentrated in prices at retail than at other levels of business, such as at the factory and in the warehouse. Because it takes all those levels into account, the deflator tended to rise slightly less than the CPI, whose complete focus is on retail transactions.

The GNP deflator is the most comprehensive inflation yardstick almost by definition—precisely because it is derived from the GNP itself, which, as we have noted, constitutes the broadest statistical measure we have of overall economic activity. Thus, the GNP deflator, at least in theory, reflects price trends throughout the country's economy, not just at the neighborhood store. Of course, we have also seen that the GNP concept has its limits, and those shortcomings, necessarily limit the accuracy of the deflator as a price yardstick.

Although the CPI and the GNP deflator are the two main means by which experts—and nonexperts—can keep reasonably up to date on general price developments within the economy, there are several other useful indexes that deserve attention. The first of these is the so-called producer-price index, which, like the CPI, is published monthly by the BLS. The producer-price index, or PPI, gives an extensive breakdown of specific items as the CPI does. The PPI , formerly called the wholesale price index, includes such categories as farm products, industrial commodities, and such "special" groups as items processed for eventual sale to consumers. The monthly PPI reports contain enormous detail about individual products. For example, under a subcategory called "non-metallic mineral products" we find this further breakdown: Flat glass, concrete ingredients, concrete products, structural clay products, refractory products, asphalt roofing, gypsum products, and glass containers and other nonmetallic minerals.

BLS statisticians break the PPI down in other ways as well. One is by stage of processing. The subgroups here include crude materials in need of further processing, intermediate materials, and finished goods. The finished-goods section is further broken down into consumer-finished goods, such as washing machines, and producer-finished goods, such as machine tools.

For all its store of price information, however, the PPI does not—in fact, by definition, cannot—provide a measurement of price trends in the service sector of the economy, an increasingly important area covered by both the CPI and the GNP deflator. Measurement of the service sector is essential to any complete view of the country's price picture. Another problem with the PPI—with which BLS officials have been wrestling—is the fact that, unlike the CPI's, its monthly prices are sometimes based on the quoted, official selling prices of manufacturers, or on prices quoted on organized exchanges or markets. The index fails to measure excise taxes or goods produced for the military, and, more importantly, it frequently fails to take into account discounts from quoted prices that are common in wholesale transactions, particularly at times when business demand may be weak. In addition, sales by the federal government to a large extent are excluded from the PPI.

Despite its shortcomings, however, the PPI does offer one important advantage over the CPI or the GNP deflator. It often tends to foreshadow trends that subsequently develop in the other two price indexes. The PPI, for instance, began dropping in late 1974 and continued to fall in early 1975, presaging an easing of the upward spiral in both the CPI and the deflator. In a very rough sense, then, the PPI can be viewed as a "leading indicator"—the term used by economic forecasters—of broader trends to come in the overall economy. There are many very much better leading indicators of general economic activity, and they will presently be reviewed in detail.

The PPI, it should be added, is one of the oldest statistical series published by the government, older even than the CPI. First issued in 1902, its initial publication covered the years from 1890 to 1901. The origins of the index can be found in a

U.S. Senate resolution, put forward in 1891, which authorized the Senate Committee on Finance to investigate the effects of tariff laws "upon the imports and exports, the growth, development, production and prices of agricultural and manufactured articles at home and abroad."

The first index was an unweighted average of 250 commodities. Since then, a system of weighting was introduced in 1914 and has been repeatedly updated, and major sample expansions and reclassifications of items have been made again and again. By the mid-1980s, about 3,200 commodities were included in the PPI, and the BLS was obtaining some 60,000 price quotations per month.

Reporting of price data by companies through questionnaires is voluntary and confidential. Most prices are collected each month, but for a few commodities whose prices change infrequently a quarterly questionnaire is used. Although price data are mainly drawn in this way, trade publications are occasionally used as well. For fish and most agricultural items, the BLS uses prices collected and published by other government agencies. Price reporting is initiated, whenever possible, by a visit by a BLS representative to the prospective respondent company. Thereafter, the mail approach is employed. The questionnaires seek detailed information centering on precise descriptions of the particular commodities, the exact basis on which particular prices are quoted, the sizes of particular orders, shipping terms, and, if applicable, discounts and taxes.

CHAPTER 4

SUBTLER SIGNS

We have seen in the previous chapter the importance of looking behind the familiar headlines that proclaim changes in such eye-catching, broad-gauge statistics as the unemployment rate, the gross national product, and the consumer-price index. Understanding something about the nature of these headline grabbers—what goes into them, their strengths and their weaknesses—constitutes a big step toward an appreciation of what the economy, that often-used but seldom-defined term, is really all about.

A familiarity with some other yardsticks—ones that make the front pages less frequently—helps provide additional perspective on the shape and nature of the economy.

LIVING STANDARDS

Knowing about the job situation or where the GNP stands or how fast the CPI happens to be climbing at a particular time doesn't tell us all that we may want to know about just how living standards across the country are faring. Is the standard of living of most Americans getting better or worse? In a sense, we are interested in the state of the overall economy precisely because we want to know what's really happening to our living standards. Unfortunately, however, there is no monthly figure produced by any of Washington's mills, or by anything else, that tells us exactly where, on a nationwide basis, our standard of living actually stands, or just how it may have changed from the preceding month or quarter or year.

Our friend driving to work may feel that his standard of living is rising or falling, depending on a variety of details possibly known only to him. His car may be bigger and more powerful than the one that he drove a year ago. Possibly he has moved to a larger house. Perhaps his salary has increased. He can afford to take his wife to dinner and the movies three times a week; a year ago such outings had to be limited to once a week. They eat steak more and chicken less. Their two children now attend private schools; a year ago they were at public schools. This year's vacation will be at Montego Bay; last year's was at Atlantic City. And this year's will be a week longer.

There no doubt are some readers who question whether our friend's standard of living has really risen at all. Who needs a bigger car, anyway? It soaks up more gasoline and is generally more troublesome to keep. Who needs steak? Our man's cholesterol count already is on the high side. Chicken might be better for his health. As for schools, it can be argued that public ones in the long run offer youngsters the best preparation for getting along in times as egalitarian as these.

It is clear that a considerable amount of subjectivity is involved when we start talking about living standards. And, as we shall see, that holds whether one considers the living standard of a particular individual, such as our friend going to Montego Bay, or of the country in general. And yet it is possible to construct a rough definition of living standards with the use of some little-publicized but readily available economic yardsticks.

One statistical series that provides such information, and the one that probably receives the most attention, is a monthly report by the BLS which shows weekly earnings expressed in constant dollars. Like the CPI, this series is broken down in various ways. It provides data by field of work—mining, construction, manufacturing, transportation, public utilities, wholesale and retail trade, finance, insurance, real estate, and other services.

The index amounts to a measure of the purchasing power of weekly paychecks of production or other nonsupervisory workers on nonfarm, private payrolls. To get at this, BLS economists first adjust gross weekly pay figures for price changes. For instance, if average weekly pay rises 10 percent but prices also rise an average of 10 percent, the price-adjusted paycheck level remains unchanged—hence the term "constant" dollars. But the BLS does not stop there. To get closer to true paycheck buying power, the bureau further adjusts the weekly average to take taxes into account. Accordingly, estimated federal income and Social Security taxes also are deducted from the gross figure.

As a result of such tinkering, we are able to obtain a much more realistic picture of the real worth of our paychecks—the amount of goods and services that they can buy—than would otherwise be the case. For example, in a reasonably representative six-year period, gross weekly pay—the dollar amount written on the average paycheck—rose by about 33 percent, but the weekly purchasing-power figure did not budge. It's not surprising that bargainers for major labor unions, if not the public at large keep a sharp watch on the purchasing power trend. It is clearly among the best measures that they have of the overall living standard of the union men and women they represent.

Like all other gauges of living standards, paycheck purchasing-power statistics must be regarded with a good deal of caution. For instance, although inflation and federal income and Social Security taxes have been removed, that is all that has been removed. Government analysts haven't yet figured a way also to account properly for state and local levies, taxes that have risen sharply in many areas of the country in recent years. This failing suggests that purchasing-power levels would be less than the published figures if such nonfederal taxes could be taken into account.

The BLS has also not managed to take into full account the so-called fringe benefits that accrue to most workers nowadays, particularly those employed by large corporations. This "nonpay pay" now runs into billions of dollars a year, and no one can pin down with certainty how many billions. How do you assign a dollar figure to a free or cut-rate round of golf at a company-owned golf club?

A study in the mid-1970s by the Conference Board, a nonprofit business-research organization based in New York, concluded that "a growing number of U.S. companies are liberalizing their employee benefits." The Conference Board estimated that "these benefits, including health and life insurance, retirement and disability income and severance pay, now account for 32.7 cents of every payroll dollar, up from 25.6 cents ten years ago." The study was based on a survey of 1,800 large corporations, representing a broad cross section of U.S. business. Because larger concerns have tended to be more liberal with fringe benefits, it is possible that the Conference Board may overstate the fringe-benefit situation for the country as a whole. Even so, the findings indicate there can be little doubt that fringe benefits constitute a large and expanding element in the standard of living of many Americans, an element that is not accounted for adequately in the purchasing-power statistics.

In any event, some economists believe that if both fringe benefits and nonfederal taxes could somehow be worked into paycheck purchasing-power data, the two missing elements would approximately cancel each other out. There can be no question that, at the least, they would tend to offset one another.

Another point to keep in mind about the purchasing-power yardstick, of course, is that by definition it covers only employed persons. At the end of 1974, for instance the weekly purchasing power of the average paycheck stood at about $89, some 5 percent below the level a year before. In that same interval, however, employment declined and the unemployment rate jumped sharply, to 7.2 percent from only 4.8 percent a year before. Clearly, the purchasing power of the overall labor force—the jobless included—fared even worse than the purchasing power of those fortunate enough to hang onto jobs.

Its limited scope is perhaps the primary reason that serious business analysts attempting to gauge overall living standards usually don't rely solely on the BLS estimates of weekly purchasing power. Fortunately, broader yardsticks of our economic living standard do exist. One is a statistic produced by the Commerce Department that shows the per-capita earnings of the country's population after all tax payments—nonfederal as well as federal—have been taken into account. Like the purchasing-power series, the per-capita income series is expressed in terms of constant dollars, with inflation removed. But unlike the BLS series, per-capita income figures take into account the entire population: Newborn babies, jobless individuals, persons who never have worked and never will, those too rich to need to work, and those too poor to work. It also embraces income from all sorts of sources besides simply the job—interest payments, stock dividends, welfare payments, Social Security payments, and the like. Indeed, it can be argued that the statistic is too wide-ranging, and that such questionable components as welfare payments are better omitted.

Not surprisingly, the per-capita income figures don't always move the same way as the BLS series on paycheck-buying power. In 1973, for example, the income statistic rose from a per-capita average of $2,931, expressed in constant dollars on an annual-rate basis, to $2,952. In the same 12 months, the purchasing-power statistic declined from about $96 weekly, again in constant dollars, to $94 per week.

Anyone trying to ascertain whether the country's overall standard of living rose or fell during 1973 would be hard-pressed to come up with a definite answer. The per-capita income figure, with welfare and Social Security payments included, would indicate a rise in living standards. But the purchasing power of weekly pay would suggest the opposite to be the case.

Perhaps the safest advice for anyone trying to gain perspective on this all-important facet of the economic scene is: Keep an eye on both statistics. It should be added that the dichotomous situation in 1973 was more the exception than the rule. It was a most difficult year to categorize, marked by severe inflation, an unprecedentedly severe Arab oil squeeze late in the year, and, near the end, a rising rate of joblessness.

Other yardsticks can also be used to gauge living standards. For instance, the BLS also issues indexes that show the buying power of hourly pay. And the Commerce Department provides data on per-capita GNP, adjusted for price changes. Neither series, however, seems as appropriate a measure of living standards as the weekly purchasing-power series or the per-capita income level.

All sorts of imaginative ways to delineate the standard of living have been devised by economists from time to time. Perhaps the most intriguing—and one that can be very easily constructed without resort to the help of a professional statistician—is something called the "discomfort index." Unlike most other yardsticks discussed but like Mr. DeVoe's CLIUI, it is not a serious economic gauge. It does help us shed light on how the nation's economy may be faring at a particular time. It is obtained simply by adding together two of the headline grabbers— the overall rate of unemployment, and the rate of increase of the consumer price index.

Looking back over the years since World War II, we see that our level of "discomfort" tended to be lowest in the 1950s, during President Eisenhower's White House years. In four of the Eisenhower years, joblessness and inflation rates, added together, came to less than 6 percent, and in two of those years the combined figure was 4 percent or less.

In many more recent years, of course, *each* of the two rates has exceeded the 6 percent mark.

Arthur Okun, a prominent economist who taught at Yale and served as a top adviser to Democratic political leaders, half-seriously picked 9 percent as the "discomfort" level—at which the country can be said to become "quite unhappy." In some recent years, exceedingly miserable ones on the economic front, the discomfort index has registered in the 20 percent range, more than double Mr. Okun's threshold for considerable unhappiness.

To gain increased perspective on the question of living standards, many economists have taken steps in recent years to try somehow to pin down elusive "social factors" in our standard of living. Efforts toward improving "social" yardsticks have been undertaken by, among others, the National Bureau of Economic Research, Inc., a nonprofit, private, business-research organization based in Cambridge, Mass., with a California office as well. The NBER, of which we shall hear more later, has launched a variety of studies aimed at devising ways to measure noneconomic elements that enter into the question of living standards. An annual report of the bureau shows studies under way by its economists "to construct indicators of health, education, environmental quality, civil rights, public safety [and] cultural participation."

The difficulty of pinning down such imponderables can be suggested by a simple example. A study by the Paris-based Organization for Economic Cooperation and Development (OECD), whose members include the major industrial countries of the non-Communist world, shows that American citizens generally have more years of education under their belts than citizens of any other major country. For example, young American workers, on the average, have completed at least 12 years of school, according to the OECD study. Close behind the United States in this admirable regard is the United Kingdom. In fact, older Britons, with nearly 10 years of schooling, on the average, actually are slightly ahead of their American counterparts. Yet other statistics, based on such purely economic yardsticks as the real GNP, show that the United States and the United Kingdom, over the years since World War II, have been among the most sluggishly advancing nations in the industrialized world. In West Germany, where the population has generally received far fewer years of schooling than in America or Britain, economic growth has been far more impressive. In terms of per-capita income, the West Germans are moving up fast on the Americans and long ago overtook the British, whose standard of living, in economic terms at least, is now one of the lowest in Europe.

But what about the relative education levels? Should the West German economic gains somehow be scaled down because their schooling appears to have been less extensive than that of the Americans or the British? And how could that possibly be done statistically? And who can say, anyhow, that seven years in West German schools are necessarily less educational and worthwhile than a dozen years in U.S. schools or ten years in British schools? Where does education fit into the picture in efforts to pinpoint living standards?

A similar imponderable is of more recent vintage. In the last several years, efforts have been undertaken in the United States, and in other countries with highly developed economies, to curb the polluting effects of industrialization on air, water, soil, and other natural resources. To its considerable credit, the United States has moved more rapidly to institute various pollution-control devices and techniques—in factories, on automobiles, at power plants—than any other major nation. This would appear all to the good, and obviously it has served to enhance, or at least preserve, the attractiveness of life in the United

States. In that sense, then, the country's living standards have generally benefited. However, in economic terms, more often than not the installation of pollution-control equipment in factories or wherever has tended to reduce the efficiency of operations. In economic terms, productivity—a matter that will shortly be discussed in greater detail—tends to be curtailed. And this curtailment, in turn, acts to limit gains in such basic economic yardsticks as the real GNP.

The paradox is readily apparent. Without efforts to keep industrial pollution under control, our living standards—economic as well as otherwise—eventually would deteriorate horribly in the smog-filled final years of this century. But the immediate effect of such efforts is to limit gains in the only statistics that we have available to show us roughly just how high—or low—our living standards may be.

The growing American effort to curtail pollution can be put into focus with a few statistics. By the mid-1970s, about 11 percent of spending by U.S. manufacturers for new plants and equipment was primarily aimed at curbing pollution, rather than at expanding output, reducing costs, or otherwise improving the efficiency of operations. In 1967, some 2 percent of such spending was aimed at pollution abatement. Thus, the share of such outlays being devoted to the basically nonproductive purpose of preserving the environment rose about fivefold. Had all those antipollution dollars been poured into highly efficient new production facilities, such economic yardsticks as the real GNP and weekly purchasing power might have made a better showing in recent years. But would our standard of living really be higher than it is today? One hardly can believe so.

EFFICIENCY

It is possible, then, to measure in rough economic terms—if not in social terms as well—the country's average standard of living. Further perspective on the overall state of the country's economy can be obtained through statistics that provide insights into the all-important efficiency with which labor and production facilities are utilized. Without improving efficiency over the years, our living standards would deteriorate in short order.

The importance of an efficient labor force was emphasized by Herbert Bienstock, a top BLS official, in charge of the bureau's big New York office. Addressing a "Conference on Labor" in New York, Mr. Bienstock stressed repeatedly that the productivity of the labor force constitutes "the key to raising American living standards." Conversely, he added, lagging labor-force productivity is "linked to a decline in living standards."

What do we really mean when we talk of labor productivity? How can we keep track of it? Why is it, as Mr. Bienstock says, the "key" to our economic standard of living?

The image of productivity that tends to prevail in most people's minds is only half right.

Simply put, productivity is—as most people believe—the measure of what a worker can produce within a specified time. Normally, it is calculated in terms of output per man-hour, or per person-hour as women's liberationists have renamed the yardstick. It is the production that results from one employee working for one hour.

However, the additional public impression—that times of high productivity levels necessarily indicate a particularly energetic, hard-working labor force and that times of low productivity imply a lazy bunch of workers—is not generally correct.

The key to labor productivity in these modern times is not the energy or enthusiasm of individual workers—though these qualities do play a role—but the efficiency of the equipment that they must operate.

To illustrate, a report by Herman Nickel in the February, 1975, issue of *Fortune* magazine noted that per-worker production of automobiles at British Leyland, the big United Kingdom manufacturer, was running at six cars annually, while per-worker car output at a comparable Japanese automobile producer was roaring along at 35 cars per year. There is no question that the Japanese labor force has generally shown more enthusiasm toward work in recent years than most British workers, or most American workers, for that matter. Some Japanese employees, for instance, delight in group-singing special songs in praise of the corporations that employ them—hardly a likely prospect in the United Kingdom or the United States. Still, by no stretch of the imagination can it be claimed that the typical Japanese auto production worker labors six times harder in the course of a year than his British counterpart—the legendary British tea break notwithstanding.

Relatively disharmonious labor-management relations in Britain are a part of the explanation. But the primary reason for the relatively high level of Japanese productivity—in autos and in most other Japanese businesses as well—is simply that Japanese workers have enjoyed the benefit of more modern, efficient machinery and other facilities than their British counterparts. Some fundamental statistics, compiled by the OECD, tell the story. Over one 13-year period, Japanese spending for new machinery and other production facilities amounted to 33.4 percent of the country's overall spending for nonmilitary purposes. In the same 13 years, output per person-hour in the Japanese labor force rose at an average rate of 10.5 percent. In the United Kingdom, in contrast, production outlays during the 13-year period came to only 18.9 percent of total nonmilitary spending, and, by no coincidence, the hourly output of British workers rose at an annual rate of barely 4 percent, less than half the comparable Japanese productivity rise.

The U.S. figures are not much better, it should be noted. Of seven major countries surveyed by the OECD, only Britain spent a smaller share on new machinery and other facilities than the United States. Of course, it can be argued that military expenditures in the United States gobbled up dollars that would otherwise have poured into streamlining civilian automobile plants, appliance factories, and the like.

In any event, the figures leave little doubt that Japanese workers are so amazingly "productive" in large part because they are fortunate enough to be equipped with relatively modern facilities.

How can we keep track of productivity in the U.S. labor force? Quite easily, if we know where to look. Again, the BLS is our main source. Each quarter, the bureau issues various indexes showing output per person-hour in private businesses. BLS statisticians compute productivity estimates using that part of the real GNP represented by private enterprise for their output estimates. This eliminates productivity "gains" really due to rising prices, and it also removes government workers, whose productivity is extremely difficult to gauge. The quarterly statistics are issued in index form, it should be noted, rather than as constant-dollar amounts. With the 1977 productivity level used as a "base" of 100, by the end of 1987, for example, productivity in private business stood at about 112; that is, the average worker's hourly output rose 12 percent in the 1977 to 1987 period. As it happens, that amounts to an increase of merely 1 percent yearly, or substantially below the average annual rise in productivity in U.S. business over the post–World War II era.

Such productivity estimates, of course, must be treated as estimates only and not taken as exact reflections of actual worker efficiency. As we have seen, the real GNP, which underlies productivity statistics, is a less than exact representation of overall economic activity. Moreover, the difficulty of precisely measuring the "output" of personnel not directly involved in turning out a product—for example, an appliance salesman at Sears, Roebuck—vastly complicates obtaining accurate estimates. This is one reason that the BLS eschews government employees in its quarterly productivity reports. How do you measure the productivity of a BLS statistician? Certainly not by the number of statistics that he can grind out each hour.

Nonetheless, BLS productivity estimates, despite their limitations, do allow us valuable insights into the overall economic situation. They are sufficiently precise to provide, for instance, a solid understanding of why, in a particular period, the country's economic living standard, on the average, may be rising or falling.

The connection that Mr. Bienstock stressed between productivity and the standard of living is fundamental. Productivity, according to Webster's dictionary, is "the ability ... to produce." In the economic world, as we have indicated, this "ability" is normally measured in terms of the amount of goods and services that workers turn out in a given period, usually an hour. Productivity gains facilitate a "better life" for workers because they tend to increase the purchasing power of paychecks. And productivity gains are essential in stopping inflation because they tend to offset cost increases due to higher pay.

If a worker get 10 percent more pay per hour but also produces 10 percent more widgets per hour, there's nothing inflationary about his pay boost, and his standard of living tends to rise. But if he gets 10 percent more pay and produces no more widgets than before, or perhaps even fewer, the pay boost can be highly inflationary, and very possibly will ultimately tend to reduce rather than improve his living standard. It drives up the employer's labor costs and puts the employer under pressure to offset the added expense through boosting prices, laying off personnel, or perhaps both.

There are many ways of illustrating the enormous economic importance of productivity. For example, an 0.1 percent speed-up in the annual rate of productivity growth can add more than $1 billion to the GNP. Unit labor costs in the 1960 to 1965 period, one of nearly inflation-free economic expansion, rose only 0.4 percent per year, on the average. But without productivity advances during those years, the average annual rise in labor costs would have topped 4 percent. Inflation would have eaten more into living standards and the growth of employment would have been much less robust.

It is no coincidence that economic living standards have risen far more rapidly in some nations than others in recent years. The leaders invariably have been countries whose productivity gains have been such that pay boosts were largely or entirely offset—and therefore rendered noninflationary—by the rising hourly output of workers. In one five-year period in the 1970s, output per person-hour in Japan rose at an annual rate of 14.2 percent. Average annual productivity gains of 5 percent and more were also recorded during the same five years in such other countries as the Netherlands, Sweden, France, and West Germany. Trailing, with productivity advancing at annual rates of only 3 percent or so, were Britain and the United States.

In Japan, and to a lesser extent in the other high-productivity countries, the productivity gains were of such a magnitude that employers were generally able to give workers hefty pay increases each year without the increases fueling inflation or causing severe unemployment. In effect, because of their rising productivity each year, these workers' living standards were able to rise as well. In the United Kingdom and the United States, where productivity gains were relatively meager during the five years, no such rise in living standards was possible.

An efficient labor force, then, contributes mightily to the health and growth of the overall economy. And worker efficiency, we have seen, can be approximately gauged through a perusal of readily available BLS data. In much the same manner, to gain the same sort of economic perspective, one can also gauge—with somewhat greater precision, in fact—the efficiency with which the country's production facilities, be they modern or relatively obsolete, are being utilized. This can be done by glancing at various surveys that estimate the potential capacity of production facilities in the United States, as well as the percentage of those facilities actually being used to turn out goods at a particular time. The percentage is aptly called by economists the "capacity utilization rate," or simply the operating rate. Perhaps the most widely followed of these surveys is one worked up monthly by economists at the Federal Reserve Board.

During the post–World War II era, for instance, such estimates of capacity utilization show that plant operations in the United States have ranged from below 70 percent to above 95 percent of capacity. The records go back to 1948. The highest rate occurred in 1951, when the Korean War placed heavy demands on U.S. industry. The rate never dropped below 70 percent until the beginning of 1975, a period of severe business distress in the United States.

The matter of precisely where, within this rather broad range, factory operations fall during a particular month yields an important clue to how efficiently the overall economy is performing. At first glance, one might suppose that periods when plant operations are very high—above 90 percent of capacity—are enormously prosperous times, marked by an economic performance of admirable efficiency. But this, strangely, tends not always to be the case. Economists have determined that when plant operations reach such high levels, efficiency actually tends to decline—production bottlenecks grow more frequent, frustrating shortages develop, costly delays in delivering goods to customers occur with exasperating regularity. Ultimately, costs

begin to go up and profits begin to go down. Given a choice—
and, of course, the ideal figure varies considerably from industry
to industry and from company to company—American manufacturers, generally, regard the area of roughly 85 percent as the
best, or in the jargon of economists the "preferred," rate of plant
operations.

A word should be inserted here with regard to the question
of how efficiently the country's overall economic facilities happen to be running at a particular moment. The Federal Reserve
capacity estimates, as well as most others like them, by definition are limited in scope to areas of the economy in which industrial products are involved. They do not cover facets of the nation's economic scene in which, for example, the "product" may
be a service rendered. To glimpse this larger picture, economists
have devised statistical estimates of what they reckon to be the
economy's potential level in terms of the real GNP, under un-
strained, healthy, relatively inflation-free conditions. Economic
operations during World War II, for example, would be viewed
as highly strained and considerably above the so-called potential
GNP level, with widespread shortages, rationing, and other
manifestations of an overloaded economy.

It is possible, using this concept of potential and real GNP,
to see how closely the real GNP figure, discussed in the previous
chapter, approximates the potential figure. It assuredly is a relationship that anyone interested in taking a closer look at overall economic performance should know about. However, the
derivation of the potential GNP figure involves some highly sub-
jective judgments on the part of economists. It is questionable
whether the levels of economic potential estimated are reasonably close to reality. The suspicion is that such capacity estimates tend to err on the high side, so that larger "gaps" show up
between the real and potential GNP figures than may actually
exist. Without getting into technical considerations, one major
reason that the economy's potential level of activity may in fact
be lower than some estimates suggest involves a controversial
question: What constitutes "full" employment in America? In ar-
riving at a figure for the economy's potential real GNP, a key
assumption has been that the country's labor force is fully em-

ployed when the jobless rate is at roughly 5 percent; lower unemployment than that, in the official view, would contribute to the sort of boomy, strained economic environment associated with times like World War II, when overall economic activity actually exceeds the potential level.

Traditionally, full employment has been the term that economists apply to the ideal situation, in which joblessness is as low as it can be without triggering serious inflation, through overburdening the country's labor resources. Years ago 4 percent was a nearly ideal level for efficient economic performance in the U.S. At the end of 1965, for instance, unemployment did in fact amount to 4 percent of the labor force. The consumer price index was rising very slightly at the time—at an annual rate of less than 2 percent—and yet economic activity was expanding at a brisk pace.

Nowadays, however, basic changes in the makeup of the overall economy, to be discussed in detail later, suggest that even a 5 percent figure for full employment may be unrealistically low. And if this is so, then the government's idea of potential GNP begins to look unduly sanguine. Economists of The Boston Company, a Massachusetts investment-research firm, worked out what the potential GNP level would have been in 1975 had the government used 4.75 percent instead of 4 percent as the full-employment rate. The Boston Company analysts came up with a potential GNP figure about $7 billion below the official figure. Their estimate suggests, among other things, that the economy in 1975 was operating considerably closer to capacity—in effect, more efficiently, but also with less of a cushion against a re-emergence of inflationary pressures—than the official record shows.

Despite its shortcomings, however, the potential GNP estimate does allow us a fuller view of the general health of the economy. In addition, it is an important concept to bear in mind when one attempts to ascertain the likely moves of economic policy makers in Washington. Suffice it to say that, when policy makers see a widening gap developing between potential and real GNP, many of them, especially the more politically-minded, become itchy to undertake measures aimed at stimulating economic activity more vigorously.

There are, of course, countless additional ways in which it is possible to gain perspective on how efficiently the overall economy may be operating. One way is to examine the economic performance from a standpoint of quality, an admittedly imponderable element that can mean different things to different people. However, periodic surveys by the nonprofit Conference Board in New York and other such economic research organizations, as well as by the government, can provide an impartial, rough idea of how well the country's production and service facilities are performing.

An example is a survey by the Conference Board of the nation's 500 largest consumer-goods companies. The Conference Board survey found that fully a quarter of the companies polled were involved in product-recall campaigns. "It is estimated that recalls will total at least 25 million product units a year throughout the rest of this decade," the report stated, and "the actual number may be even larger, since there are thousands of unreported recalls." The survey also found that "the number of product liability suits is growing swiftly, with hundreds of thousands of grievances—real and imagined—being filed in city, state and federal courts." From a strictly economic point of view, the study went on, the rash of recalls poses some major "hazards," because the trend "could place many small and medium-sized companies in extreme financial jeopardy." The trend also indicates, of course, a rise of slipshod, inefficient work in American factories and elsewhere. It is an aspect of our economic health that simply can't be determined by merely perusing data on operating rates or the size of the GNP gap.

AS OTHERS SEE US

In a delightful poem called "To a Louse," Scotland's great eighteenth-century poet, Robert Burns, wrote:

> O wad some Pow'r the giftie gie us
> To see oursels as others see us!
> It wad frae mony a blunder free us,
> And foolish notion.

The statistical yardsticks discussed so far in this book have represented ways of looking at the economy from a largely national perspective. When we look at figures that bear on the labor situation or production levels or price levels or living standards or productivity, we view the economy not in broad world terms but in a strictly U.S. context. We can determine whether the real GNP, for example, went up or down in a given period, and how rapidly. But to gain the broadest possible perspective on the trend, whatever it may be, it would help to be able, as Robert Burns observed in pondering a very different situation, to be able to see ourselves as others see us. In our personal lives, as the poet suggested, the feat may be well-nigh impossible. But in trying to assess the nation's economy, there are ways to gain a bit of external perspective.

A brief mention has already been made of international comparisons. We have seen, for instance, that worker productivity in Japan has tended year after year to outpace productivity gains recorded in the United States. We also have seen that it is possible to put into international perspective such matters as the share of U.S. spending that goes into new machinery and other production facilities. Other such comparisons can be made, using a wide range of economic measures, from GNP data to CPI data, available in moderately reliable form. Many of these will be discussed in a later chapter.

In addition, there are several yardsticks that can be readily used to catch a glimpse of our economy as it appears to others. Like other economic measures reviewed in this chapter, these internationally oriented yardsticks rarely command big headlines. But anyone who takes the trouble to follow them will obtain a broader view of the general health of our economy.

One such yardstick is the country's international balance of payments. As the name implies, the balance of payments is derived from the record of financial transactions that take place between the United States and the rest of the world during a particular period. Issued on a quarterly basis by the Commerce Department, the balance-of-payments statement covers receipts and payments involving both private and government transactions, whether settled in cash or financed by credit. It includes, for example, merchandise trade, tourist expenditures, sales of military equipment, and interest and dividends deriving from international investments.

The balance-of-payments statement helps us gain a broader view of our economy because it gives us a look at America's financial standing vis-à-vis the rest of the world. If we see, for example, that the country's balance of payments in a particular quarter is in surplus, this normally suggests, in world terms, a relatively healthy U.S. economy. It indicates that, in its overall business dealings with other countries, the United States is managing to take in more money than it must pay out. The precise reasons for the surplus can be found in a breakdown of the Commerce Department's quarterly statement. We may find, for example, that large inflows of foreign funds occurred because goods made in the United States were in particularly strong demand around the world, or because many foreign investors decided that the time seemed right to plow large amounts into companies based in the United States. In either event, the implication is that the U.S. economy is relatively attractive and healthy.

Conversely, a balance-of-payments deficit normally signifies that the country's economy is performing relatively poorly in world terms. It may be that foreign-made merchandise is winning U.S. customers away from American-made goods, as happened through much of Ronald Reagan's presidency. It may be that foreign investors take a skeptical view of investment opportunities in the United States while American investors would rather put their resources into business projects abroad than at home. Whatever the case, the pattern does not inspire confidence in the condition of the U.S. economy.

A further word should perhaps be said about that part of the international balance of payments that has to do with trade. For good reason, almost as much attention is paid to the balance of trade by serious economic analysts as to the overall balance of payments.

The country's trade balance is simply the relationship between its exports and its imports. If U.S. trade with the rest of the world is in surplus, this obviously speaks well for the international competitiveness of U.S-made goods. If a deficit occurs, it suggests that U.S. products aren't faring well in the world marketplace. Some business analysts feel that by concentrating on the country's trade balance, rather than on its overall payments balance, they can get a clearer, simpler reading of the U.S. economy's international standing. They contend that the overall payments figure can be too wide-ranging, just as we have seen that GNP estimates can be too wide-ranging. The balance-of-payments position, for example, can be affected significantly during a given quarter by flows of funds that represent merely speculative efforts to make a quick profit on interest-rate differences between the United States and other countries. Such "hot money" flows are hardly a true indication of the economy's basic well-being.

Trade figures, in contrast, normally offer a straight-forward sign of how the country's products are stacking up against those of other countries. This is a major reason why America's trade figures are deemed far more significant than their size would lead one to expect. U.S. exports, for example, have amounted in recent years to roughly 10 percent of the country's GNP, far less than the comparable percentage in most industrialized lands.

Without going into the full record here, it is important—and disheartening—to observe that both the U.S. balance of payments and the U.S. balance of trade were extensively in deficit in many recent years, not surprisingly years that must go down as generally dismal ones for the nation's economy.

There is another important international yardstick that can help us to see our economy as others see it—the international value of the American dollar. At any given moment, we can readily determine how much the dollar in our pocket is worth in terms of a particular item that we may wish to purchase. All we have to do is venture into our local supermarket or clothing store to discover precisely how much our dollar can buy. But this will not tell us a great deal about the dollar's value in the rest of the world. It won't tell us what foreigners think of our dollar. We may find that our dollar can buy more food in the supermarket this week than last week because food prices have dropped; its value within the context of the local supermarket has increased. But it may be that although our dollar's buying power at the supermarket has risen during the week, its international value during the same seven days has fallen. It may buy more bread and peanuts, but it also may buy fewer Swiss francs or West German marks or Dutch guilder at banks and other business places where one country's currency may be exchanged for another's.

Many of the economic statistics that we have discussed thus far, and many of the important economic indicators that we will presently take up, are denominated in dollars, some adjusted to take the country's inflation rate into account, as we have seen, and some not adjusted for inflation. Such statistics, adjusted or unadjusted, can be assessed more meaningfully if one also is aware of how the dollar stands internationally.

Like a deficit in the balance of payments or the balance of trade, a prolonged decline in the value of the dollar in terms of other currencies normally suggests a relative weakness in America's economic situation. The reason could be, for instance, that international investors feel there are better opportunities for their funds elsewhere and therefore have little need to acquire U.S. dollars with which to buy into U.S. projects. Ultimately, the supply of dollars will tend to exceed the demand for dollars in international dealings, and the dollar's international value will tend to sink.

A glance at the important matter of productivity, for instance, helps illustrate further why it is so vital to keep the dollar's international value in mind while studying many economic statistics. As noted, productivity gains in the United States in one five-year period trailed the corresponding increases in Japan and various other industrialized nations. However, the U.S. productivity performance appears still more dismal if one takes into account the fact that the U.S. dollar's value during the period declined sharply in terms of Japanese yen and most other currencies of countries whose gains in productivity were significant. During the five years studied, as reported, the hourly output of U.S. workers rose at an average annual rate of only about 3 percent. But the BLS bases such estimates on hourly output figures denominated in dollars. What the BLS does not—indeed, cannot practically—take into account in its productivity figures is the international value of the dollar. During the five years in question, it was declining sharply in terms of most other major currencies.

If the BLS had recalculated its estimates of U.S. hourly output in terms of, say, yen, that 3 percent annual rise in U.S. productivity during the period would have evaporated. Instead, a decline in productivity would have occurred.

It obviously is too much to expect the BLS and other issuers of important economic statistics to recalculate all their dollar-denominated statistical indexes in terms of various foreign currencies. On the other hand, it is a relatively simple matter for the interested layman who wishes to gain a broader view of the U.S. economy to bear in mind that there is a second way of looking at many important economic yardsticks—by viewing them against the background of how strong or how weak the dollar may be in international currency markets at the time in question.

To wit, an economy in which productivity is rising 3 percent annually and the dollar is weak is a much less impressive one than an economy in which productivity is rising 3 percent annually and the dollar is strong.

CHAPTER 5

UPS AND DOWNS

A cycle, according to the Merriam-Webster dictionary, is "a period of time occupied by a series of events that repeat themselves regularly and in the same order."

It is necessary to appreciate something about cyclical behavior to gain a fuller understanding of what we mean when we talk about "the economy." In preceding chapters, we examined several of the more significant yardsticks that economists have devised to provide snapshots, as it were, of overall economic activity. We saw how such widely followed measures as the unemployment rate, the gross national product, and the consumer price index are put together and may be used—with caution—to glimpse the general economic picture. We also examined a variety of less well known statistics, from paycheck-purchasing power to productivity to balance-of-payments data, that provide additional perspective on the state of the economy.

A fuller understanding of the economy necessitates not only a familiarity with these yardsticks. It also requires an appreciation of how the economy tends to move. Like waves in the sea or flames in the fire, the economy is in constant motion. The statistical yardsticks that we scrutinize for economic perspective are constantly changing. A fuller understanding of the economy entails an understanding of how it moves.

It is a striking sort of movement. Research extending back over more than 130 years—well before Civil War days—shows that the economy moves in a cyclical fashion. In line with the dictionary definition of a cycle, the economy has tended to move in a manner that repeats itself in an orderly sequence. This cyclical behavior can be seen in economic record books, whether one chooses to peruse data involving jobs or the GNP or prices or any one of many other economic gauges.

Impressed by the cyclical nature of economic activity over the years, economists have managed actually to pinpoint, within each economic cycle, distinct phases—alternating periods of expanding and then contracting economic activity. These phases have been pinpointed down to the precise months in which each began and ended. Periods of expanding economic activity, appropriately, are referred to as *expansions* or *recoveries*. Periods of contracting activity are called, also appropriately, *contractions* or *recessions*. The end of each expansion phase is marked by a distinct *peak,* as economists call it. The end of each recession phase is marked by what economists call a *trough.* The level of economic activity has risen greatly over the years because, quite simply, the expansion phases have been overwhelmingly longer, on the average, than the periods of contraction.

As one might expect, the expansion periods are marked by increases in such wide-ranging gauges as the gross national product and by declines in such others as the unemployment rate. Conversely, recession periods usually witness a climb in the unemployment rate and a drop in the gross national product after adjustment for price changes—the real GNP, as described earlier. In noninflationary times, it should be noted, the GNP itself, as well as the so-called real GNP, has also tended to shrink during recessionary phases of the business cycle.

A brief review of the up-down movement of the economy over many decades should help to underline how cyclical the pattern has been.

RECORDS

Economists of the National Bureau of Economic Research, the nonprofit business-research organization based in Cambridge, undertook many years ago the task of pinpointing these ups and downs of business. To determine the precise peaks and troughs, they have used—and continue to use—not only such headline-grabbing yardsticks as the GNP and the unemployment rate but scores of other statistics. Some of these others are measures already discussed in detail, such as prices and productivity. Others will be reviewed in due course. Still others, including highly arcane statistics guaranteed to befuddle and bore most laymen, and perhaps some economists as well, need not be delineated here.

The National Bureau has managed to chart this cyclical pattern of the economy all the way back to 1854, about as far back as the research organization dares to go without having to rely on statistical data whose accuracy, to put it mildly, may be questionable.

The cyclical behavior of the economy seems so well established that analysts automatically take it into account when they try to estimate the future business course. In early 1975, a time of worsening recession in America, with unemployment rapidly rising and the real GNP plunging, Albert Cox of Lionel Edie argued that better times were down the road because—simply—"the business cycle is working its way toward recovery." In other words, recessions inevitably are followed by recoveries.

Economists occasionally do come along who, out of an optimistic nature or merely ignorance of economic history, convince themselves that the economy's cyclical behavior has somehow become outdated, that healthy economic growth can be sustained indefinitely through diligent policy-making, and that nasty, recurrent recession periods are avoidable. In this regard, I can still recall an encounter in the mid-1960s with Otto Eckstein, a young Harvard economics professor who at that time was serving as a member of the President's Council of Economic Advisers, a panel of three economists charged with providing advice on economic policy to the country's chief executive, who then was Lyndon B. Johnson.

The encounter occurred in New York City, just after Mr. Eckstein had addressed a large conference of business executives, a well-heeled audience that seemed delighted with the economist's highly optimistic appraisal of future business developments. The overall economy at the time had indeed been expanding for several years, after a recession that ended in early 1961. Understandably, recession memories had been getting distant and dim. Some economists, including Mr. Eckstein, were beginning to talk boldly about a new era dawning in which the economic course could—and would—be made smoothly expansionary year after year after year. Recessions, to these sanguine analysts, were merely a memory from the benighted pre-1961 past.

Unconvinced, I had recently written an editorial in *The Wall Street Journal,* where I served at the time as economic news editor. Among other things, the article suggested that anyone, from President Johnson on down, who believed that the business cycle was dead and buried, and recessions with it, might be in for some rude surprises in the years ahead. The article apparently attracted the attention of Mr. Eckstein, a notably sanguine member of Mr. Johnson's economic team. Accordingly, when we happened to meet in New York, the Presidential adviser turned to me and, fixing me in his bespectacled gaze, inquired loudly: "You don't really believe that stuff you wrote the other day about a recession coming along, do you? " Rather than engage in a public debate with a high-ranking Washington official, I chose the cowardly path and, mumbling an unintelligible response, quietly removed myself from the circle of business executives who were mingling around the diminutive professor, mostly to express their admiration for his cheerful, recession-free appraisal of economic prospects.

As both Mr. Eckstein and I soon saw, the business cycle lives. The expansion phase that was well under way when he gave that optimistic address in New York persisted only until 1969, when a recession set in that lasted for one year. Since then, of course, the ups and downs have kept coming. As pointed out, the National Bureau's record-keeping of these cycles, in extensive detail, begins with 1854. According to the bureau's estimates, a business-cycle trough occurred in December of that bygone year. The ensuing recovery phase continued for a full two and a half years, until a business-cycle peak was reached in June 1857. The subsequent economic contraction from this peak lasted until December, 1858, an 18-month recession. That is unusually long for a recession, according to National Bureau records. Then another up-phase in the cycle started, until a peak was reached in October 1860. That 22-month expansion was followed by an 8-month recession, which in turn was followed by a 46-month expansion phase that encompassed the Civil War.

Altogether, the record indicates that since that first expansion phase began in December 1854, there have been 30 expansions, up to the long one that began in late 1982, and an equal number of recessions. The National Bureau, whose analysts tend to be extremely cautious about such matters, generally doesn't label expansion or contraction phases of the business cycle until many months after the fact. This procedure allows the Bureau ample time to collect, scrutinize, and reflect upon scores of economic statistics, some of which are slow to be compiled or are subject to repeated revision. For this reason, only in 1975 did National Bureau analysts come around to setting a precise trough date for the recession that ended in late 1970. The month that they finally picked was November.

A summary of the business cycles determined by the National Bureau since 1854 shows, among other things, that through the 1981 to 1982 recession, the expansion phases averaged 33 months and the contraction phases 18 months. The longest expansion on record was the aforementioned 1961 to 1969 expansion, which lasted 106 months. The second-longest expansion on record was an 80-month upturn in 1938 to 1945. The third-longest was a 58-month upswing in 1975 to 1980. And next, somewhat strangely, was a 50-month upturn that ran from 1933 to 1937, a period of double-digit unemployment. The National Bureau's record-keeping, it should be explained, focuses strictly on whether the economy has been in an up-phase or a down-phase. Thus, one of the longest periods of economic expansion in the country's history occurred during the country's worst depression. Of course, the economy was rising from horrendous depths. The real GNP, among other key yardsticks, did not regain its pre-depression level before a new down-phase set in during 1937. The shortest expansion phase on record was a 10-month upturn in 1919 to 1920.

As for business downturns, the longest was not the famous 1929 to 1933 collapse; that lasted a long 43 months. The longest contraction of economic activity took place between October 1873, and March 1879—altogether a miserable 65 months. The shortest recession on the books lasted only six months, in the first half of 1980. The next shortest, seven months long, occurred in 1918 to 1919.

Both those short recessions, it should be noted, occurred in wartime. National Bureau records, in fact, give scant support to arguments that the U.S. economy needs wars to keep expanding. Five recessions, in all, have taken place partly or entirely during wartime. In addition, the records show that some of the longest periods of expansion took place in peacetime. The record-breaking 1961 to 1969 expansion is classified as a wartime upturn by bureau analysts. However, the healthiest growth during that expansion actually transpired before the United States became deeply involved in military operations in Vietnam.

National Bureau data also show how the various expansions and recessions compare in terms of vigor and weakness. The length of a particular phase has not always been a useful indication of its character. For example, an extremely short slump in 1945, only eight months long, was marked by a 35.4 percent plunge in industrial production, while a 13-month recession in 1926 to 1927 was marked by a drop of only 7 percent in industrial production. By the same token, the 50-month economic expansion of 1933 to 1937 can hardly be remembered as a period of business vigor. Far more vigorous, for instance, but shorter, was the 45-month expansion of 1949 to 1953.

What the long record since 1854 demonstrates, through all the varying expansions and contractions, is the cyclical way in which the economy tends to expand. It is like the walker who gets to his destination ever so slowly by taking two steps forward and then one backward.

Wesley C. Mitchell, who headed the National Bureau in its early years, and Arthur F. Burns, the Federal Reserve Board Chairman who followed Mr. Mitchell as head of the bureau, attempted to define the cyclical nature of business in a 1946 paper. In part, they concluded, "a cycle consists of expansions occurring at about the same time in many economic activities, followed by similarly general recessions [and then] revivals which merge into the expansion phase of the next cycle."

A 1962 study by the Federal Reserve Bank of Philadelphia

also stresses the cyclical nature of economic growth. The Philadelphia bank emphasizes that this cyclical behavior entails two
kinds of economic growth—rapid growth during expansion
phases of the business cycle, and long-term growth that accu-
mulates over decades—in part because expansion phases are, in
general, much more durable than contraction phases.

The bank puts the situation this way: "Sometimes the economy could be said to be underweight. Sometimes it is operating
below its capacity and output tends to stagnate. A significant
proportion of factories and machines are not in use and unemployment is high. The immediate need is to grow back to the full
employment level. Although some may not think of it as such,
this is desirable growth . . . because if more people go to work,
there should be more goods and services produced for each person in the country to enjoy." The bank then proceeds to describe
long-range economic growth: "The other kind of growth is more
of a long-range thing. It could be compared to the way a child
grows taller by building bone and muscle. In economic terms, we
could say, it is increasing the nation's overall ability to produce."

In summary, the bank states: "Where the first kind of
growth is filling out to use existing capacity, the second kind
means adding to that capacity. And it also results in more output
per capita because each worker becomes more efficient and is
able to produce more goods and services. Both kinds of growth,
of course, may happen at the same time, and it is often difficult
to distinguish between them."

It is possible, using statistics with which we already are familiar, to see over the very long pull what level of growth this
cyclical behavior of the economy has produced. Perhaps the best
statistic for the purpose is the real GNP. Government estimates
show that the real GNP in this century has grown at an annual
rate of close to 3 percent per year, on the average. Growth of
industrial production, another broad-gauge measure of the economy that reflects the physical output of the nation's factories,
has grown somewhat faster—about 4 percent annually—over
the same span. The discrepancy can readily be explained. The
industrial production yardstick, which is compiled by the Federal Reserve Board on a monthly basis, does not encompass services, which of course go into the real GNP figures. Because ser-

vice industries—not to be confused with service-type jobs—have expanded less rapidly since 1900 than manufacturing industries, this has tended to hold back long-term expansion of the real GNP. A major reason that service growth has lagged, simply, is that the use of high-speed, increasingly efficient machinery is mainly of benefit to the economy's industrial sector. How do you automate a haircut? How do you speed up open-heart surgery? To put it another way, the relatively slow long-term growth of services reflects considerations unrelated to the short-term ups and downs of the business cycle.

In fact, a close inspection of how various segments of the economy normally behave during times of recession shows that services hold up relatively well. It is industrial production, with its relatively high long-term growth, that generally contracts severely during recessions. Of course, the industrial sector also generally expands extra sharply when a period of economic expansion gets under way. A prime example is the highly important, highly volatile automobile industry. In good times, the industry expands car production at a fierce pace, and when times turn bad few industries cut back output more severely or, generally, appear more distressed.

REASONS

Thus far in this chapter, we have inspected the way in which the economy moves and, in the process, grows. The historical research of economists at the National Bureau, in the government, and elsewhere has enabled us to look back over the decades, for more than a century, and observe the ups and downs of business activity. It has allowed us to scrutinize the dimensions of any particular business cycle with regard to all sorts of data—average number of hours worked weekly, average price of 500 leading common stocks, the dollar volume of business spending for new plants and equipment, the number of new housing units under construction, and on and on.

The plethora of statistical information is useful in dozens of ways, from enabling the interested layman simply to keep a more intelligent tab on the highly complex movement of the overall economy to permitting all sorts of investors to make all sorts of investment decisions—some wise and some not so wise—about where to put their money.

However, a question remains: Why does business exhibit this cyclical behavior? What forces underlie this up-down tendency that seems to persist—to prevail—despite the best-intentioned efforts of policymakers, men like Otto Eckstein, to guide the economy smoothly along an expansionary path?

The aforementioned study of the Philadelphia Federal Reserve Bank finds a good deal of downright mystery in this up-down pattern of business growth. Indeed, its analysis is titled "The Mystery of Economic Growth." The impetus for economic expansion in large measure derives, when all else has been analyzed, "from some inner spark," the Philadelphia bank concludes, adding that "we don't know exactly how it works and until we do, it is wise not to overlook such 'old-fashioned' things as initiative, drive, incentive, motivation, confidence, and the willingness to invest."

We still do not know completely "how it works." But there are important observations that can be made. First, the nation's economy is basically founded on a system of private enterprise that even in this day of "big government" is only guided and not rigidly controlled by federal, state, or local planners. Private planners, be they shopkeepers or the chairpersons of vast corporations, can err—on occasion as disastrously as government planners sometimes err. They can make bad decisions. When things are going along well, they occasionally neglect the sort of cautionary business procedures that, paradoxically can keep things going along well. When things are going badly, they occasionally neglect to take gutsy measures that can improve the situation in the long run. In brief, business decisions, whether made in Washington or in New York City or in, say, Salisbury, Connecticut, are made by human beings—and human beings make mistakes.

To this essential consideration must be added the fact that our economy—like the economies of major industrial nations generally—comprises, to a very large extent, businesses that deal in manufactured goods. This list ranges from such important items as automobiles, appliances, and heavy machinery to a countless array of less significant merchandise. These goods must be fashioned in factories, using such basic materials as steel, copper, and coal. They then normally must be distributed and eventually sold to customers throughout the United States and abroad. If factory operations are properly geared to demand, so as not to overproduce or underproduce particular items, business generally should tend to prosper and, in the long run, expand. After all, the U.S. population continues to expand, albeit at a reduced rate. In addition, technological progress tends to bring higher worker productivity, and this too should foster faster economic growth; as we have seen in an earlier chapter, rising productivity and rising living standards generally go hand in hand.

Over very long periods, these forces—an expanding population and an increasingly productive work force—do indeed promote economic growth. Without such trends, that close to 3 percent yearly increase in the real GNP this century would simply not have been possible. However, the economic decisions that underlie the production, distribution, and sale of the sundry items that pervade the marketplace cannot be tailored precisely to ever changing patterns of demand. Business planners, in other words, can never be so wise as to preclude a cyclical pattern in the movement of the economy.

In practice, manufacturers generally do try to keep a close watch over the inventory situations of their wholesalers, who in turn generally do try to keep abreast of the inventory positions of their many retail outlets. In recent years, computers have no doubt facilitated such efforts. But mistakes continue to be made. Morris Cohen, former chief economist of Schroder Naess & Thomas, a New York investment research concern, provides a reasonably typical example of how thoughtful business analysts view the role of inventory policy in the larger business-cycle picture: "While inventories represent a small fraction of the total economy, big swings in inventory changes have typically provided the main reason for business cycles."

When business is going well, business planners sooner or later make the error of overestimating the prospects for further economic gains, inventories pile up, workers must be laid off, and we wind up with a recession. When business is not going well, business people tend to believe that the depressed state of affairs won't ever end. It eventually does end, of course. Inventories are worked down. But business planners, still in a recessionary mood, are slow to gear up to meet burgeoning customer needs. Eventually, they must scramble to catch up—and we get economic growth far above that long-term rate of 3 percent. Indeed, we all too often get economic growth that is too rapid and brings with it shortages, overstrained production, and, sadly, painful inflation.

This recurring tendency to overestimate and underestimate was driven home to me many years ago when, as a young reporter in Chicago for *The Wall Street Journal,* I was responsible, among other ignominious duties, for covering conventions that major appliance dealers held annually at Chicago's vast Merchandise Mart. My practice was to buttonhole as many dealers as possible during the two or three days available and ask them quite specifically how business was faring at their respective dealerships. After I had collected perhaps 40 or 50 such hallway interviews, I would try to put it all together into a trend-catching feature article for the paper, summarizing the state, at least at the retail level, of the U.S. appliance industry. The dealers proved to be remarkably candid with me, to the point where they would freely disclose such information as how their individual sales and profit margins compared with levels, say, a year earlier.

Reviewing my notes from such interviews, I began to notice an extraordinary pattern. In years when the appliance business had generally been good, for example, the dealers would generally tell me that business was "good." But then, ever the intrepid appliance reporter, I would press on and ask whether sales in the last few weeks or months were actually running as much ahead of rates a year before as, say, had been the case six months earlier. And more often than not, the ebullient fellow who had just informed me how "good" his business was would hesitatingly report that well, as a matter of fact, sales in the past few weeks were actually no higher than last year's comparable level, or maybe, now that you mention it, just a shade below it. And, if I pressed a bit further, more often than not I would find that the fellow's inventories, now that the matter came up, had taken an unexpected jump in the past month or so and were appreciably higher than a year before. "No doubt a fluke" was the usual comment.

The same sort of pattern emerged, in reverse, when the dealers were interviewed after a year or so of poor business. Invariably, the initial response would be that business was indeed "lousy." But further questioning, more often than not, would turn up a report that sales, while perhaps still lagging, were not lagging quite as badly as a month or two ago, and that inventories, while still excessive, were somewhat leaner than a few weeks ago.

In the end, it was a tricky undertaking to decipher what these appliance dealers had to report. For usually their initial pronouncements about the business picture turned out, on close questioning, to be almost wholly backward-looking. And, of course, my journalistic task was to provide *Wall Street Journal* readers with an idea of what might lie ahead, rather than what lay behind, in the nation's appliance business. Complicating the job even more was the fact that the dealers tended, I noticed, to tailor their planning—buying appliances from wholesalers, expanding outlets, and so forth—to their experiences over the past year or two, rather than to recent sales and inventory developments.

I recall an especially frustrating series of interviews in early 1960. Invariably, the dealers at first would tell me—and I am certain they meant it—how great things were. But then it would develop that, yes, inventories were climbing sharply and, no, sales in the last three or four weeks actually weren't above year-earlier levels; in fact, they were dipping a little below year-earlier levels. Eventually, I produced for the paper a quite gloomy appraisal of the appliance business that bore scant resemblance to many of the general statements of optimism jotted down in my notebook. The headline, I recall, was: "Appliance Anxiety—Worried Dealers Cut Prices as Sales Lag, Inventories Pile Up."

The story, which appeared in January 1960, proved—as things eventually turned out—worth the effort. It was among the first to suggest that the economy, which had been expanding, might be starting to turn sour. In fact, the expansion under way at the time shortly ended and a bona fide recession began in April 1960.

Is it any wonder, I later thought, remembering the ebullience of those appliance dealers, that our economy periodically seems to get ahead of itself and winds up in a recession?

There is a footnote to the story that seems, in retrospect, worth adding. To round out the article, I telephoned a few appliance manufacturers, to supplement the views of the dealers. I found, to my astonishment, that most of the manufacturers, far from cutting back their production schedules in line with swelling inventories and slackening sales at the dealerships, were sharply expanding output. I recall, for instance, that the Gibson Refrigerator division of Hupp Corporation was setting its first-quarter production schedule for a whopping 57 percent increase over the corresponding 1959 rate of output.

When the story appeared under the gloomy "Appliance Anxiety" headline, it caught the eye of the chief executive of one large maker of appliance parts, who also happened to be a director of Dow Jones & Company, *The Wall Street Journal's* corporate parent. He was so upset by its gloominess that he took up the matter with the head of Dow Jones. His market research people, the appliance executive told the Dow Jones head, foresaw a very good year and thought that the pessimistic tenor of that article by the young fellow out in Chicago was totally unjustified. The Dow Jones boss, to my great relief, suggested that we all sit back and let events take their course. The director never apologized to me. But why should he have? He provided me with an unforgettable illustration of how very nearsighted business planning, even in supposedly well-run, blue-chip corporations, can occasionally be.

As long as there is an appliance industry—never mind automobiles—there will be economic ups and downs.

In this chapter, I have observed that private planners do occasionally err, and the attitude of that Dow Jones director, I believe, underlines the point. The further suggestion has been made that government planners display a fallibility fully matching that of their private counterparts. A later chapter will detail the impact of Washington policy-making on the economy in general. An appreciation of the ups and downs of business, however, requires some mention at this point of the governmental role. The government, as noted, attempts to guide the economy in a manner conducive to steady, rather than erratic, expansion. The effort is mainly conducted through fiscal and monetary measures. Such measures involve government spending, taxation and, through the Federal Reserve Board, regulation of the nation's money supply. The last is a most important but little understood facet of the economic picture, to be taken up at length later.

If the human beings who make policy efforts in Washington were wondrously wise, their policy might succeed so well that optimists like Otto Eckstein no doubt would be proved correct—the economy actually might expand, without recessionary interruptions, year after year after year. The wisdom in Washington would be sufficient to offset stupidity displayed perennially at the Merchandise Mart, in corporate boardrooms, and elsewhere throughout the private economy.

But the reality of the situation is not like that. The economic policies formulated in Washington all too often prove not to be carefully and wisely constructed. And, as a result, they do not foster the sort of recession-free economic growth that would obviate business cycles. Indeed, a strong argument can be made that Washington's efforts in the recent past to eliminate the cyclical behavior of the economy may inadvertently have intensified the up-down tendency. It may be no coincidence that one of the sharpest recessions on record developed in the early 1970s, on the heels of a decade in which many Washington officials apparently convinced themselves that they really could place the economy along a permanent path of recession-free expansion.

Tilford Gaines, chief economist of Manufacturers Hanover Trust in New York City, once said this about such Washington attitudes: "The middle years of the 1960s were a time when [policy-making] economists took an almost arrogant pride in their ability to control the U.S. economy. Policies were evolved . . . that led economists to believe they could 'fine-tune' our economic progress. . . . The economists' arrogance of the mid-1960s not only was unfounded but contributed to the difficulties that the economy later encountered."

Mr. Gaines suggested that there is an "apparent need for humility on the part of government officials, economists and others in their manipulation of . . . policy to steer the economy." The Manufacturers Hanover analyst concluded that "the changes in fiscal and monetary policy over the past 10 years have been intended to be economic stabilizers" but have in fact had the opposite effect.

Such criticism, it should be stressed, is by no means unique. Another critic is A. Gilbert Heebner, for many years chief economist of Philadelphia National Bank. He echoes Mr. Gaines in his view that "our experience has been that government authorities are not skillful at regulating economic policy and that they usually overdo restraint or stimulus."

To sum up, ineptitude (coupled often with arrogance) in Washington has tended to exacerbate the economy's natural tendency to move in a cyclical pattern. A case in point is the performance of the Federal Reserve Board, supposedly immune from political pressures, with its seven governors appointed by the White House for 14-year terms. The Fed has again and again failed to promote the sort of steady, moderate growth in the nation's money supply—on the order of 3 percent to 5 percent yearly—that many economists estimate would be appropriate for an economy with resources such as ours. Instead, Federal Reserve monetary policy has fluctuated wildly, from periods of excessive expansion, with monetary-growth rates above 10 percent, to harshly restrictive periods in which the money supply actually has dwindled. The Federal Reserve's refusal or inability to regulate monetary growth more evenly—the explanation is not clear-cut—will be taken up more closely later. For the moment, suffice it to say that the up-down movement of the economy in general is matched, at the least, by fluctuations on the monetary front.

The efforts of the White House and Congress to control economic growth through fiscal measures—spending and taxing— seem often, like the endeavors of the Federal Reserve, to accentuate, rather than reduce, the cyclical movement of the economy. The White House and Congress tend, of course, to be far more sensitive to political pressures than the governors of the Federal Reserve Board, with their super-long terms. And popular demand has generally favored avoiding at almost any cost the widespread joblessness that prevailed during the 1930s. Accordingly, the tendency of the men who have occupied the White House since World War II and of Congress has been to support legislation producing—at least in the short run—more jobs. Usually, the job creation has entailed increased spending. The tone was set with the passage of the Employment Act of 1946, a short but to-the-point item of legislation stating, in essence, that the country's leaders should place job creation as their number one priority on the economic front.

The trouble has been that the fiscal stimulus has come in fits and starts, ill-timed, and often beyond the economy's digestive powers. It can be argued, for example, that the recession of 1969 to 1970 was actually hastened and aggravated by efforts in the mid-1960s, led by President Johnson, to cut taxes while concurrently increasing spending, not only for the supposed domestic welfare but to pay for the intensifying war in Vietnam. The inflationary strains that subsequently developed in the economy—for example, sky-high loan rates—served to inhibit further economic growth, and in fact set in motion some of the very forces that led to an eventual recession.

The fact that much of the spending rise was for military purposes acted only to aggravate accumulating inflationary pressures. The reason, simply, is that spending dollars, say, for bombs puts more money in the hands of thousands of workers in military bomb factories. But it does not increase the supply of goods available for consumption. It does nothing to provide more washing machines or refrigerators or other such items that bomb production workers may wish to buy with money earned making bombs. The upshot is a situation in which inflationary pressures can intensify with extraordinary speed.

Though the cyclical nature of economic growth largely derives from the behavior of business planners in and out of Washington, there are outside factors that do, occasionally with a vengeance, influence how underlying patterns may develop. An example is the oil squeeze that the Arab countries imposed on the United States and other major oil-consuming countries in the fall of 1973. It is generally agreed that the U.S. economy was still in an expansion phase, which began in late 1970, when the oil squeeze developed. How much longer that expansion phase would have continued had the Arabs not cut the oil supply is a matter of conjecture. Forces already were developing in the fall of 1973—for example, an excessive accumulation of inventories in many businesses—that would surely have eventually led to an expansion peak and a subsequent phase of contracting economic activity. But there is no question that the jolting reduction in Middle Eastern oil supplies, with the long lines at gasoline stations and the occasional curtailment of production at fuel-short factories, hastened and very possibly deepened the recession.

Geoffrey Moore, a Columbia University economist as well as the National Bureau's top consultant on business-cycle patterns, estimates that the recession began in November 1973, when Arab oil supplies were being curtailed. It is impossible to say precisely when the recession would otherwise have occurred. But the general view is sometime in 1974. My personal estimate is August 1974, roughly the time such broad gauges of economic activity as the unemployment rate and the real GNP began weakening severely.

AND A FOOTNOTE

The ups and downs of the economy that already have been discussed and will continue to draw our main attention are not the only fluctuations detected over the years by economists. They are, for the purposes of this book, far and away the most important. However, it should be mentioned that other cyclical patterns have been observed from time to time by economic researchers. These divide, roughly, into very long ups and downs, so-called super-cycles extending over decades rather than only a few years, and very short down-phases within the larger expansion phases of a normal business cycle. These have been christened, somewhat ridiculously, *growth recessions*.

Neither of these phenomena seems clearly enough established, in my view, to warrant extensive discussion. Nor does either appear particularly useful in enabling us to keep a reasonably intelligent watch over the daily unfolding of major economic developments—if you will, over the headline grabbers. Still, a footnote may be in order simply to prevent possible confusion about the ups and downs of the economy staked out by the National Bureau of Economic Research.

Let us first briefly consider the super-cycle idea. There are at least several variations. These generally hold that above and beyond the normal cyclical pattern of economic growth there exist super-cycles within which the expansion and contraction phases thus far discussed represent mere ripples. Perhaps the most intriguing super-cycle concept is the so-called Kondratyev Wave. The name refers to the late Nicolai Dmitrievich Kondratyev, a Soviet economist whose major writings appeared in the mid-1920s. He subsequently was shipped off to Siberia, where he labored in salt mines for many years and finally died.

The idea behind the Kondratyev Wave rests to a considerable extent on the Soviet economist's studies of long-term price movements, particularly with respect to agricultural items. The Russian concluded from his extensive research that business activity actually takes on a rhythmic, wavelike pattern over extremely long intervals. Using price indexes and other economic yardsticks, mainly available for such relatively advanced countries as the United States, Britain, and France, Mr. Kondratyev theorized that "super" business cycles exist. A super-cycle, according to the Russian's theory, extends over periods averaging roughly fifty years. One Kondratyev super-cycle transcends many "short-term" ups and downs that the National Bureau charts.

Underlying the Kondratyev Wave idea is the assumption that a very high degree of inevitability governs economic developments over many decades—that governments, for instance, can possibly delay but not entirely eliminate periods of "correction" that inevitably must follow periods in which economic growth reaches excessive rates.

The Kondratyev Wave theory can be applied to the U.S. economic record, going back at least to the late eighteenth century. Prices—and prosperity—increased markedly from the 1780s until just after the War of 1812, when a sharp price decline occurred. This period constituted, under Kondratyev theory, a "primary" recession within a super-cycle. Then, until about 1819, a "plateau" period persisted in which prices declined only moderately and economic activity seemed to recover somewhat. But after that a deep "secondary" slump set in. Prices and business activity declined sharply for a prolonged interval marked by high joblessness and spreading bankruptcies. The bottom did not come until the mid-1840s. Then a super-cycle expansion phase ensued, reaching a super-cycle peak around the end of the Civil War, half a century after the War of 1812.

Kondratyev theory contends that after the Civil War peak a super-cycle pattern developed remarkably similar to that after the War of 1812—a short primary recession, then a plateau until 1874, a prolonged secondary slump until 1896, and finally a span of renewed prosperity and rising prices until 1920.

The price collapse and 18-month recession that began in July, 1921, according to the Kondratyev Wave theory, marked still another primary recession within a super-cycle. The balance of the decade witnessed a plateau period. The Great Depression, until the late 1930s, marked a secondary-slump phase. A renewed expansion stage then developed, according to Kondratyev disciples. The recession that hit the economy in 1981 to 1982, which turned out to be the harshest slump since the 1930s, represents still another primary recession, in the Kondratyev view. It remains to be seen what will develop on the economic front as the decade of the 1990s dawns. If Kondratyev theorists prove correct, the years just past constituted a relatively trouble-free plateau period and should be followed by, alas, still another horrendous secondary slump.

Such ideas hardly add up to a sunny view of a capitalist economy. Yet, a vital part of the Kondratyev Wave idea is that the down-segments of each super-cycle serve as a sort of self-cleansing mechanism and establish a foundation from which renewed, vigorous economic growth is possible. Largely, it is this aspect that upset Stalin and led the Communist dictator to banish Mr. Kondratyev to Siberia where, according to Aleksandr I. Solzhenitsyn in *The Gulag Archipelago,* the Russian economist ended his days in "solitary confinement, became mentally ill there and died."

The *Bank Credit Analyst,* a monthly economic report of a

Montreal investment advisory concern, has noted that the Kondratyev idea has been attracting more attention of late. The explanation, it believes, is not complicated: "What has created a renaissance of Kondratyev Wave theory is, first, the intuitive feeling among a growing number of people that we have over the postwar period pretty well milked our economic system by pushing debt loads to the limit and that from here on we must deflate one way or another."

Against such considerations, to be sure, must be weighed a variety of factors that seem to point in the other direction. The Kondratyev Wave, for example, assumes a flexibility within the economy, so that the aforementioned self-cleansing process may occur. However, as the *Bank Credit Analyst* concedes, "wages are almost totally inflexible now, whereas they tended to fall in previous deflations" observed when Mr. Kondratyev was formulating his concepts. By the same token, the Russian could not have envisioned the extent of government intervention—often of an inflationary nature—that nowadays permeates economic affairs even in staunchly non-Communist countries.

It can be argued, accordingly, that Kondratyev ideas are hopelessly out of date. It can also be argued, however, that the very inflexibilities that may seem to invalidate Kondratyev could, in coming years, produce inflation so ruinous that a Kondratyev-like secondary slump could develop in the inflation's wake. Whatever does develop, it is surely an interesting footnote to any study of economic growth that the controversial ideas of Stalin's Siberian prisoner are still alive. In the next chapter, we will take up the subject of how the economy has indeed been changing over the years, quite apart from the cyclical behavior already discussed.

Before proceeding to the matter of super-short cycles, it should perhaps be emphasized that the Kondratyev Wave is merely the longest of a variety of very long economic cycles, real or imagined, that various analysts have discerned when poring over economic records in the United States and abroad. There are also, for example, so-called Kuznets cycles, named for Simon Kuznets, an economist who taught for many years at Harvard. These cycles, which seem to range up to about 25 years, or barely half as long as Kondratyev cycles, are characterized particularly by swings in construction activity. Economists who have studied evidence suggesting super-long business cycles cite many possible underlying factors. They range from wars to the effect of gold discoveries on world monetary growth to inventions to immigration trends to long-term weather trends and their impact on food production.

The idea of very short cycles—actually economic dips within the expansion phase of a normal business cycle—is of relatively recent vintage. Solomon Fabricant, a senior economist at the National Bureau, has attempted to pinpoint these intervals, which he calls growth recessions. He lists, for instance, as many as three such intervals between 1961 and the end of the 1960s, a period marking the longest expansion phase in the National Bureau records back to 1854.

Bona fide recessions, as noted, are characterized by actual declines for at least a half year or so in such yardsticks as the real GNP and industrial production. Growth recessions, in contrast, are merely intervals within expansions in which the real GNP, for example, tends to rise relatively sluggishly. Like super-long cycles, these super-short growth recessions are mainly matters for debate among economists and are not normal grist, certainly, for page-one economic news.

The growth-recession idea, in any event, is responsible for at least one amusing, no doubt apocryphal, story about Mr. Fabricant. It comes from Herbert Stein, a genial economics professor who served as chairman of the President's Council of Economic Advisers under Richard Nixon. Mr. Stein, who clearly feels that there are weightier economic questions to concern business analysts than growth recessions, reports having seen Mr. Fabricant out walking a dog one evening.

"What a nice dog that is," Mr. Stein claims to have remarked.

"Why, this is no dog," Mr. Fabricant replied, according to the story. "It's my growth horse."

Whatever political considerations may underlie Mr. Stein's telling of the story—he understandably did not enjoy hearing the word "recession" in any form while he served in the White

House—the point seems valid. A dog is a dog and a horse is a horse. And an expansion, it would appear, is an expansion. To begin trying to find tiny ups and downs within all the larger ones—which are difficult enough to track—seems almost as ridiculous as calling a dog a horse.

CHAPTER 6

CHANGES, FOR BETTER AND WORSE

An understanding of what we call "the economy" necessitates a familiarity with trends that in the long run can deeply alter its nature and performance.

There is, we have seen, a sameness about the manner in which general economic activity expands and contracts, expands and contracts. The up-phases have exceeded the down-phases, and so the economy has grown. In addition, during the long span of cyclical growth, significant changes have occurred in the makeup of the economy. Its internal dimensions have been changing while the economy as a whole has been expanding. An appreciation of these internal changes helps further to broaden our perspective.

The changes, slowly developing over decades, can be seen in a variety of ways from a variety of vantage points. Economic activity, as reported in the previous chapter, has been expanding over the very long pull of this century at an annual rate of about 3 percent. But growth within the economy—within the sundry components of the gross national product—has not been even in the least. Some components of the GNP have lagged and others have spurted swiftly ahead, far more rapidly than the whole. As a result, the composition of the overall economy—the relative importance of particular facets of the GNP—is notably different nowadays from its composition 20 or 30 or 40 years ago. Understanding what has been happening provides an important insight into the economy now.

Let us begin the examination using the GNP data mentioned briefly in the third chapter. And let us focus our attention first on the remarkable transformation that has occurred with regard to the relative importance of private and governmental activity.

UNCLE'S GROWING ROLE

The statistics that go into the GNP make it possible to glimpse how the government's importance has expanded over the years. We observed in the third chapter that major components of the GNP include consumer spending, business spending, government spending of various sorts, and, small but nonetheless important, foreign trade results. We noted approximately how much each of these components contributed to the GNP—in effect, to overall economic activity in the country. We saw that the largest of these components is the category that embraces consumer spending. It accounts for something close to two thirds of the total. And we saw that government expenditures are a distant second, accounting for something under a third of the total. The breakdown leaves little doubt that the consumer remains "king" of the American economy.

However, none of this tells anything about changes that may be occurring—important, long-term trends—within the economy. GNP statistics in considerable detail are available back into the 1920s, and even a cursory glance at the record shows, above all else, the steady expansion of the government's economic role. It is a remarkable trend. In 1929, the GNP amounted to $103 billion and government expenditures totaled less than $10 billion: in terms of the overall economy, this spending was under 10 percent. It is occasionally assumed that the advent of World War II caused the first major expansion in the government's economic role, and that the much-publicized New Deal programs of President Franklin D. Roosevelt did little, in fact, to alter the economy's basic makeup. This is not correct. In 1940, well before Pearl Harbor, government spending was already over $14 billion, while the GNP, at $100 billion, was actually under the 1929 level. In terms of the GNP, government outlays in 1940 came to substantially more than the 1929 level.

During World War II, of course, the government's share of

the GNP soared, exceeding 40 percent in 1944. But that was an aberration that hardly helps clarify the long-term pattern. A jump to peacetime 1960 is more instructive. By then, the GNP stood at $515 billion, more than five times the prewar 1940 total. But government spending in 1960 exceeded $100 billion, seven times the comparable prewar level. In terms of the GNP, government spending in 1960 came to about 20 percent.

Since 1960, the government role has continued to expand. And the long rise, significantly, seems to transcend political divisions. The climb before World War II occurred largely in years of Democratic leadership in Washington. But the rise on to 1960 cuts across eight years of a Republican president. Recently, of course, the rise has persisted under three more Republican presidents, all avowed opponents of "big government." The rise has gone on in peacetime as well as in wartime.

What sort of spending by the government has led the increase? What has lagged?

In 1929, when government expenditures amounted to about $10 billion, the bulk of that total—$7 billion—represented spending not by Uncle Sam in Washington but by state and local authorities. Such nonfederal spending traditionally has gone largely into salaries of public-school and college teachers, policemen, firemen, garbage men, and the like, and into school construction, mass-transit facilities, and other regional projects. In 1940, although overall government spending, at $14 billion, was well above the 1929 total, the state-local component stood at only $8 billion, only $1 billion higher than 11 years earlier. In 1960, with overall government spending up to $100 billion, some seven times the 1940 level, the state-local component stood at $46 billion, less than six times higher than in 1940.

Over the years, then, government spending has expanded far more rapidly than economic activity as a whole. And within this fast-growing segment of the GNP, spending by the federal government has risen even more rapidly than spending by states, counties, cities, towns, and other nonfederal authorities.

The GNP statistics also provide a breakdown of federal expenditures—between military outlays and other spending. In prewar 1940, the record shows, military outlays amounted to about a third of all federal spending. But in 1960, it was over two thirds of the total. The rate has since dropped, which is a reflection that the sharpest expansion within the swiftly expanding federal sector has been elsewhere than in the much-criticized military arena. It has been, mainly, on the domestic front, which encompasses the broad field of social welfare. To gain a better insight into the sort of economy that has evolved over the decades of general expansion, it is worth examining the remarkable growth of this segment of federal spending more closely.

To appreciate what has happened, it is useful first to become acquainted with a term that rarely makes the headlines: *transfer payments*. If spending by the federal government has risen far faster than any other major segment of the GNP, it is largely on account of transfer payments. They have soared.

What are they?

Simply defined, transfer payments are government transfers of money, acquired chiefly through taxation of business concerns and working people, to individuals who render no service in return for the funds received. Transfer payments include Social Security payments and other government-sponsored pension-type programs, unemployment benefits, food stamps, welfare payments, and various federal health-care and health-insurance benefits.

As recently as 1965, these governmental transfers of income from producers to nonproducers amounted to $42 billion, or less than 12 percent of wages and salaries paid out that year to working Americans. In 1975, a scant 10 years later, transfer payments soared past the $103 billion level, nearly five times the 1965 total. Transfer payments approximate 25 percent of wage and salary payments to workers. President Gerald Ford warned in 1975 that Americans might encounter a time in the not-too-distant future when half the working-age population would, in effect, be working to support, through their tax payments, the other, nonworking half. The rise of transfer payments is obviously what the President had in mind.

The boom in transfer payments, it should be added, has gone on during expansion phases as well as recession phases of the business cycle. Admittedly, 1975 was affected by a severe recession. But economic activity rose substantially between, say, 1972 and 1973. Yet transfer payments rose in both periods. In 1972 to 1973, they increased from $113 billion to $130 billion.

The expanding role of transfer payments within the overall economy has major ramifications. Quite apart from obvious sociological considerations, the trend has profound economic significance. Whether, on balance, it represents a welcome or unwelcome economic development is a subject of great controversy. Understanding this controversy facilitates a greater general appreciation of the current economic situation.

An editorial in *The Wall Street Journal* in early 1975 expressed the serious misgivings of some observers about the trend. "While the payments are of course defended on the grounds of compassion," the editorial states, "they are having a serious effect on the economy, by steadily breaking down the relationship between reward and effort." The article goes on to warn that "private production can no longer carry the burdens placed on it by government." The editorial concludes: "The nation has been flirting with the breaking point for a long time. ... Present and future taxes, which have to be raised to finance government deficits, are now so high that it is more beneficial for more and more producers and workers to not work than to work."

The situation may or may not be that bleak. But there is no denying that the average worker's tax burden has increased mightily, just as transfer payments have increased mightily. This is made clear, for example, by a Conference Board report showing, among other things, that federal income-tax payments in a recent 10-year period jumped 170 percent. The report also shows that tax payments eat up twice as much of the average individual's income as they did 25 years earlier. Social Security payments, a major component of transfer payments, soared nearly 300 percent during the 10 years, the Conference Board further reports.

Evidence that transfer payments are rising even faster than taxes prompts observers who worry about the trend to stress another point. They express concern that the country's political leaders, who ultimately shape general economic policy, perennially are quick to sanction further transfer payments but always seem notably slow to sanction any tax boosts that might be needed to muster funds *for* transfer payments. This reluctance, it is argued, tends to make the economy more inflation-prone. When insufficient taxes are collected to cover rising government payments, the shortfall must be made up largely by increasing the nation's money supply—a move that can be accomplished through various actions of the Federal Reserve Board.

In any event, the argument runs, such increases in the money supply tend to be inflationary. They tend to drive up prices. In effect, the government prints money, which it then hands out to Social Security recipients, people on welfare, and other nonworkers. But these nonworking recipients, somewhat like the people mentioned in Chapter Five who work in bomb factories, do little or nothing to increase the supply of goods and services available for consumption. It is an elementary rule of economics that prices will tend to rise along with the supply of money when there is no concurrent rise in the available supply of things to spend the new money on.

Accordingly, it can be argued that the rise of transfer payments within the overall economy—whatever the benefits may be—has altered the economy's nature in unfortunate ways. The rise has made the economy more prone to inflation. It has tended to limit the productivity of those who work and invest by burdening them with disheartening tax obligations. It has given able-bodied nonworkers little incentive to bestir themselves.

Analysts who worry about the rise of transfer payments within the overall economy often cite Britain's troubled economic scene as an example of where the trend can lead. Transfer payments—and the high taxes that go along with them—may or may not be at fault in Britain. It is true, however, that Britain's economy has turned in an exceptionally feeble performance over the postwar era. It is also a fact that transfer payments loom exceedingly large in the British economy. A breakdown shows, for instance, that Britain's "social contract"—in large part, transfer payments for health and welfare—amounts to roughly 80 percent of per-capita income in the country. By no coincidence, the income-tax rate in Britain—despite some recent cuts—runs to higher levels than in many industrial countries and is hardly designed to spur individual incentive and hard work.

It remains a question whether Uncle Sam is on the same road as John Bull, in regard to transfer payments or economic feebleness. But some analysts, distressed by the rapid rise of transfer payments in the United States over the years, fear that this may be the case. If so, they foresee a U.S. economy that may perform far more sluggishly and be subject to far worse bouts of inflation than has heretofore happened. The cyclical pattern of growth will no doubt persist. However, with incentives to produce diminishing, the up-phases may become much weaker, and down-phases, exacerbated by inflation, may prove more severe. Over the long pull, some analysts fear, economic expansion may prove much more difficult to achieve. That long-term growth rate of 3 percent yearly, some believe, may become impossible to maintain in the years ahead.

A key ambition of Ronald Reagan's presidency, to be sure, was to reduce tax rates and thus inspire greater work incentives and, along with this, greater productivity and ultimately a broad rise in general living standards. But the overall tax burden, despite repeated rate cuts, didn't drop. In fact, data compiled by the Tax Foundation, a nonprofit research group based in Washington, show that in the latter years of Mr. Reagan's White House tenure the number of working days required for the average U.S. taxpayer to "earn" his tax obligations was growing. In fact, the number was longer in 1988—with "paid-up day" as late as May 5—than before Mr. Reagan took office in 1981. The early years of his presidency did witness a brief decline, with the paid-up day as early as April 30. But this trend soon reversed, partly reflecting the rise of state and local tax obligations as the top federal rates went down.

In sum, it can be argued that the Reagan administration's plan to spur economic activity never really received a fair test. The fact is that productivity gains through much of the Reagan era were lackluster. In addition, of course, huge federal-budget and foreign-trade deficits piled up, casting shadows over the country's long-term economic outlook, and government spending repeatedly reached new highs. It amounts to a strange, depressing showing for a president advertised to be a fiscal conservative determined to "get the government off our backs."

But there is another, very different side to the coin, and it also should be examined for a full appreciation of how Uncle Sam's expanding role, through transfer payments, may influence the economic picture. This side of the coin appears considerably less gloomy. It involves, essentially, the idea that transfer payments, far from hindering long-term economic growth, serve as a vital economic safeguard in recessionary times, when business activity may threaten to contract too severely. Indeed, the swelling role of transfer payments is at the heart of arguments that an economic scenario similar to or worse than the experience of the 1930s is most unlikely. Nowadays, the argument holds, a worker may be laid off, as in the 1930s, but, thanks to transfer payments, his purchasing power continues, albeit at a somewhat diminished pace. Because there is no drastic elimination of purchasing power nowadays, it is claimed, a super-severe, snow-balling collapse of consumer demand is prevented. In brief, down-phases of the business cycle are automatically prevented from getting too deep.

This argument is put forward by an impressive array of analysts. An analysis of the long-range economic significance of transfer payments has been made, for example, by the economics department of Pittsburgh National Bank. "Increases in such payments help individuals to maintain income levels and have an important role in mitigating decreases in consumer spending," the analysis states, adding that "transfer payments expanded rapidly in every post-World War II recession—as unemployment grew, unemployment-insurance payments automatically expanded."

The Pittsburgh bank goes on to observe that Uncle Sam is by no means the sole source of such recession-fighting funds. Reviewing developments during the recession that began in late 1973, the report notes that many states changed their unemployment-insurance laws in 1974 and early 1975 to increase benefits. Some extended unemployment insurance coverage to include state employees, as well as to farm and domestic workers. Some also repealed provisions denying benefits to pregnant women. Minimum weekly benefits were increased in many states and eight mandated a maximum benefit equal to two thirds of the state-wide average weekly wage. A number of states, in addition, repealed the one-week waiting period for receiving benefits. In several states, moreover, the first week was made compensable after a claimant was unemployed for a specific period. A number of states lengthened the duration of benefit payments. "Most changes in unemployment insurance are in the direction of increasing payouts to individuals," the bank's analysis concludes.

Unemployment benefits are not the only type of transfer payments that have risen sharply. Social Security payments and Medicare payments are on the list, along with others.

The bank's conclusion, it should be added, is clearly approving of the trend. "Unemployment compensation is one of the nation's built-in stabilizers," it declares. "During a period of generally falling business demand, production is curtailed by reducing hours and employment, as producers adjust to current levels of ordering. The unemployment that results from an output cutback and reduced sales produces a markedly lower level of overall personal income. Unemployment insurance payments and other transfers help to cushion the downward income effects of a decline in business activity. The cushioning effects of transfer payments by governments to persons means individuals, as a group, will have more purchasing power than otherwise. Everything else held constant, consumers will be able to spend more and the decline in business will not be as sharp or last as long as it would without the various benefit payments."

A similar view emanates from the economics department of New York's Citibank. "At the onset of the Depression," the bank has stated, "there was very little by way of governmental machinery to provide income for the unemployed, the aged, the disabled and the dependent young. Now, income-maintenance programs, while far from ideal, mitigate suffering."

Such views of the economic impact of transfer payments clearly clash with the relatively pessimistic argument that such income transfers tend to retard the economy's progress, weakening expansion periods and intensifying inflationary pressures. It is impossible to say unequivocally that one view or the other is correct.

THE SWING TO SERVICES

Other highly significant changes in the nature of the economy can be glimpsed in the GNP data. One that is far subtler than the surge of transfer payments, but no less important, involves the expanding role of services. Consumers devote a larger share of their budgets nowadays to services. And, by no coincidence, a rising fraction of the work force toils in service-type jobs.

Recent statistics show that approximately 53 cents of each dollar spent by American consumers is spent for service items— ranging from haircuts to TV repairs to electricity to rent to maid service. Until 1968, consumers consistently spent more on so-called nondurable goods than on services. In 1967, for example, consumer spending for services came to $216 billion, while consumer spending for nondurable items totaled $217 billion. The main components of the latter category are food, of course, clothing, and oil and gasoline, whose prices soared after the Arab oil squeeze in late 1973.

The pit of the Great Depression marks a period, it should be noted, in which service outlays also accounted for a very large share of consumer spending, though not as large as these days. But unlike nowadays, the predominance of service spending during those troubled times stemmed not from any surge in such expenditures. Rather, it reflected the fact that spending for service items—particularly such essential items as rent and health care—simply fell more slowly than spending for most goods.

The durable-goods category, whose key components are automobiles, furniture, and appliances, fell particularly sharply during the Great Depression, plunging from $9.2 billion in 1929 to a low of $3.5 billion in 1933. Obviously, in bad economic times, it is easiest to postpone the purchase of a car or refrigerator.

Along with the swing to services in consumer budgets has come a still more dramatic swing to services on the job front. The rise in service-type jobs, of course, reflects in part the rise in spending for service items. It also reflects the spectacular ability of America's farms to turn out more food with fewer people tilling the soil—thanks largely to giant advances in the fertilizer and farm-equipment industries.

But that is only part of the explanation. Service-type jobs

have proliferated in recent years within companies that are essentially manufacturing concerns. The production-line employee is still there, for instance, at the auto factory. But now, backing him up at headquarters, are many more clerical personnel than was the case years ago.

The reason isn't simply that we live in a period of expanding red tape and paperwork—though this is a factor. We also live in a period of increasingly efficient machinery. People on the production line grow increasingly productive—unlike their colleagues pushing papers at headquarters. Productivity in service-type jobs is not so easily increased. To repeat a familiar question: How do you automate a haircut? The upshot is that service-type employment, largely impervious to the techniques of automation, has soared in relation to production-line jobs in recent years.

Some years ago, Victor R. Fuchs, a senior economist at the National Bureau of Economic Research, produced a remarkable study of this labor-force development entitled "The Service Economy." The 280-page report describes in detail the growing role that services play in the U.S. economy and suggests how this growth may shape American business in coming years. One result of the rise of services, he reports, is that the United States has become the first nation in history where more than half of the working population—over 60 percent—is employed by organizations that provide services rather than goods. Moreover, Mr. Fuchs reports that nearly all the country's employment growth in the decades since the end of World War II has been accounted for by jobs opening up in the service area.

The implications of the swing to services, in Mr. Fuchs's view, are broad indeed. He compares it with "the transition from an agricultural to an industrial economy, which began in England and has been repeated in most of the Western world." In some respects, the implications of the transition to a service-oriented economy are "revolutionary," the National Bureau analyst claims. One plainly economic implication, suggested in other studies of the general trend, is that services inject an element of stability into the economy. "Services cannot be stored," Mr. Fuchs writes. "Thus, this sector avoids the swings in output that result from changes in the rate at which business firms and consumers add to or diminish their inventories of goods." As the importance of services increases, the economist believes, "we can expect more stability."

A somewhat surprising implication of the swing to services, Mr. Fuchs claims, involves its possible long-term impact on the role of corporations. A common belief is that corporations will continue to expand and gain more power in coming years. But the emergence of an economy heavily oriented toward service industries militates against this assumption, Mr. Fuchs says. The manufacture of goods, he notes, is mostly accounted for by "large profit-seeking corporations." In the service sector, on the other hand, "firms are typically small, are usually owner-managed, and are often noncorporate. Furthermore, nonprofit operations, both public and private, account for one-third of the service sector's employment."

Mr. Fuchs cites statistics showing that the role of big corporations as employers has recently declined. "We may see an end of the myth of the dominance of the large corporation in our society," he declares. "Most people do not work and never have worked for large corporations [and] in the future the large corporation is likely to be overshadowed by the hospitals, universities, research facilities, government agencies and professional organizations that are the hallmarks of a service economy."

The rise of services, in the view of Mr. Fuchs and other prominent analysts, also presents a challenge to big labor unions. "More than half the persons employed in industry are union members," he notes, while the service sector "is only about 10 percent unionized." As a result, he contends, "unless there are strenuous new efforts at organization, the continued growth of services may mean a decline in union influence in the United States." Recently, such a decline has grown increasingly evident.

Efforts have been made by labor leaders since Mr. Fuchs's analysis to organize more service-type workers. But their success seems limited.

A 1975 study by the Conference Board finds that "the rise in union membership has not kept pace with the growth in nonagricultural employment." In a recent 10-year period, the Conference Board reports, union membership—though up about 17 percent in absolute numbers—dwindled in terms of overall employment. It fell to 26.7 percent of the work force from 29.8 percent and is now below 20 percent. "The manufacturing sector of the economy has been and continues to serve as the foundation of the American labor movement," the report states. "Employment in this sector, however, has remained relatively stable, even though total nonagricultural employment has risen. Hence, though roughly half the manufacturing work force is organized, as a proportion of all organized labor, it declined to 42.8 percent from 46.6 percent" during the 10 years. The study indicates that the rise in jobs has come in the service area, where union organizing hasn't been nearly sufficient to offset the long-standing aversion of most service-type employees to joining a union.

The rise of services within the economy, clearly, has tended to reduce the percentage of the labor force that is unionized. But this does not mean that potential inflationary pressures due to labor costs have been reduced. It is a fact that unionized workers generally are able to drive a harder bargain with employers at the negotiating table than nonunion employees are able to achieve independently. But it is also true that unionized workers tend to be, as we have observed, in jobs where productivity can often be sharply increased through the use of more efficient machinery. Thus, sharp pay increases in such jobs don't necessarily mean higher labor costs—or higher prices for consumers. In many nonunion, service-type jobs, on the other hand, productivity gains are difficult, if not impossible, to achieve because such jobs often don't entail the use of machinery. The upshot is that relatively small pay boosts in such jobs can push up employers' labor costs—and ultimately what the consumer pays—more strongly than sharp pay increases won by, say, unionized workers in the highly mechanized steel industry.

In sum, productivity gains constitute a major offset to rising pay levels—and productivity gains generally come harder in service-type jobs, where unionization is relatively scarce, than in production jobs, where unionization is widespread. Accordingly, the swing to services in no way signals an easing of inflation due to labor-cost pressures. And, if unions grow more successful in signing up service workers, labor-cost pressures could sharply intensify.

UNHAPPY TRENDS

The nature of the economy has been changing in other important—and unfortunate—ways. These other trends may prove ephemeral, or they may become more pronounced. One such change, already briefly noted, and painfully apparent to laymen as well as economic experts, is that the economy seems to be getting more inflation-prone. Over the very long pull, prices generally have risen. Using the 1967 average as a base of 100, our old acquaintance the consumer price index in 1979 pushed above the 217 mark and in 1987 crossed the 345 level. Again using 1967 as a base, the recent level amounts to more than five times the CPI level that prevailed early in the post–World War II era.

The change that has been occurring on the inflation front, however, isn't simply that prices have climbed greatly since early in the century. It is that in relatively recent decades the inflationary tendency has grown more pronounced. The CPI, among other price yardsticks, has risen far more rapidly in the last 35 years, for example than in the 35 years before that. Prices naturally do tend to rise during brisk expansion phases of the business cycle and fall in sluggish recession phases, largely in response to supply-and-demand forces. However, in recent decades this tendency has greatly diminished. Prices generally have continued to rise most sharply around the peak of expansion periods, but they also have tended to keep right on rising, albeit more slowly, in recessions. The upshot is that the long-term rise in prices has recently accelerated.

A few statistics show the emerging pattern. During most of the 1948 to 1949 recession, the CPI did indeed decline, and the price index dropped again in the 1953 to 1954 recession, though less sharply. In the next post–World War II recession, in 1957 to 1958, the CPI dipped only briefly, however, and it actually rose over the full course of the slump. In each of three subsequent recessions, the index rose persistently and with increasing intensity. In fact, in some months of the slump that began in late 1973, and again in the 1981 to 1982 recession, the CPI climbed at double-digit annual rates.

Many economists have devoted a great amount of their time trying to ascertain precisely why the economy seems to be more inflation-prone nowadays. There are, unfortunately, no easy answers, and any attempts to explain the development invariably provoke considerable debate, which typically divides along political and philosophical lines. A few reasonable observations can be made, however. One involves the relationship between money and prices. The word "inflation," according to Webster's dictionary, refers to "an increase in the volume of money and credit relative to available goods, resulting in a substantial and continuing rise in the general price level." One trouble has been, in the view of some analysts, that the volume of money and credit has indeed been rising too swiftly in recent decades—far more rapidly, in fact, than the availability of goods and, we should add, services. This concern has been voiced by Richard T. Selden, an economics professor at the University of Virginia. Writing in a monthly economic survey published by Morgan Guaranty Trust Company, in New York, Mr. Selden states: "One causal element has accompanied every inflation the world has ever known: expansion of the money supply at a faster rate than output growth." He goes on in the article to detail at length the speedup in monetary growth—and in the price climb—in recent decades. For example, he divides a 16-year period into two eight-year segments, 1957 to 1965 and 1965 to 1973. The money supply rose 25.2 percent between 1957 and 1965, he estimates, and 57.8 percent between 1965 and 1973. Turning to prices, he finds that the general price level rose 13.2 percent in 1957 to 1965 and 42.5 percent in the more recent period.

The professor bluntly blames the nation's monetary officials for, in effect, printing too much money and thereby causing a severe worsening of inflation. He calls this an "unfortunate 'greening' of America," of a very different sort than the widely publicized "greening" that Professor Charles Reich of Yale wrote about years ago. Mr. Selden calls the overproduction of money the "real greening of America" and blames it not only for worsening inflation but for many other economic ills.

The accelerating rise of the money supply has been accompanied, other statistics show, by an accelerating increase in the amount of credit pervading the economy—the other inflationary ingredient mentioned in Webster's definition. The climb of credit in the post–World War II era has been to say the least, extraordinary. Just since 1970, until 1988, total debt owed by all levels of government, all private corporations, other organizations, and individuals has risen from 1.3 times the gross national product to 1.7 times the GNP. The inordinate expansion of consumer credit has been carefully tracked by John Gorman, a senior economist in the Commerce Department. In the early postwar years, Mr. Gorman reckons, the average American had to use about 10 percent of his after-tax earnings to service accumulated personal debt—paying for interest charges and amortization of outstanding loans. Recently, this ratio, which Mr. Gorman calls the consumer's debt-service burden, has been close to the 25 percent level.

Corporate debt has risen even more steeply than consumer debt. Arthur Burns of the Federal Reserve Board once called the drastic increase in corporate debt—with its inflationary implications—the nation's "number-one" economy worry. Also on the rise, though less sharply, has been government debt. Altogether, total debt in the economy now tops $8 trillion, up from less than $1 trillion in 1960.

Another ingredient in the economy's growing susceptibility to inflation involves a consideration quite apart from the climb of money and credit. It is the proliferation of regulations, often government imposed, that generally serve, among other functions, to keep prices from dropping when normal economic forces would otherwise cause them to drop. Thomas G. Moore, a researcher at Stanford University's Hoover Institution, has compiled a list of some two dozen such governmental "barriers," as he labels them, to greater price flexibility within the economy. Some are of long standing, but others are of more recent vintage. The list has been lengthening. It includes, for example, a variety of costly subsidies paid to producers of all sorts of agricultural products.

"Government programs should be designed to lower prices and to make the economy more flexible, rather than to create barriers" to competition, Mr. Moore declares. "Yet, a wide variety of government programs, both legislative and administrative, have worked to raise prices or costs." Efforts to arrest this trend, made in the Carter and Reagan administrations, have been of little avail.

Mr. Moore does not happen to mention other legislation and rules that allow monopolylike power to a handful of huge, industry-wide labor unions. As Victor Fuchs has made clear, there appear to be distinct limits to the power and growth of unionism in an increasingly service-oriented economy. Still, there can be no question that, in certain key industries, union power has added fuel to inflationary forces. Looking back over the general wage record during recessions, it is readily apparent that in the most recent recessions, by and large, hourly wage rates kept right on climbing, while in earlier slumps wage rates often declined—along with labor costs and, ultimately, the general price level. Unions, even in construction and other industries troubled by relatively high joblessness, will rarely entertain the idea of reducing wage rates in order to open up more jobs. Wages in such industries have become, in the jargon of economists, inflexible on the down-side—and so, it seems, have prices.

The economy's increasing susceptibility to inflation isn't the only unhappy change in recent years. The economy also appears to be more prone to unemployment, perhaps for some of the same reasons that inflation has been worsening. As reported in Chapter Three, the much-publicized unemployment rate is a somewhat misleading reflection of actual conditions within the labor force. There are serious questions about the way in which figures on the jobless rate are compiled. Moreover, as noted previously, such factors as minimum-wage laws tend to make the U.S. job picture appear relatively bleak. But none of this adequately explains the fact that, like inflation, unemployment in the U.S. has tended to grow progressively more severe.

Unemployment, like inflation, tends to respond to changes in the business cycle. The unemployment rate drops to relatively low levels around peaks of expansion phases and rises to relatively lofty levels around troughs of recessions. However, unemployment has tended, in recent decades, to improve only sluggishly during expansions and to become unexpectedly severe in recessions. In the recession that began in 1973, for instance, the unemployment rate reached the highest level—9 percent of the labor force—since the bad old days of the Great Depression. The rate went higher still in the 1981 to 1982 recession, crossing above the 10 percent mark. In the 1969 to 1970 recession, by comparison, joblessness never exceeded 6 percent of the labor force. Still more noteworthy, unemployment has grown increasingly sticky in good times. In the first long expansion after World War II, in 1949 to 1953, unemployment dropped well below 3 percent of the labor force. In the next major expansion, 1954 to 1957, the rate fell below the 4 percent mark. But in more recent expansions, it has rarely been that low. In the 1970 to 1973 economic upturn, the rate managed to edge only below the 5 percent level and then but briefly.

Clearly, more is involved here than methods of statistical compilation and long-standing minimum-wage regulations. One factor, which will be discussed more fully later, is the increasing competition that American workers face from workers abroad, whose wage rates often may be below those of their U.S. counterparts. In the early years after World War II, the clear superiority of American production facilities generally allowed U.S. workers, despite vastly higher pay levels, to compete with great success in the international marketplace. Now, of course, war-ravaged industries abroad have been rebuilt and streamlined. Relatively high U.S. wage levels can no longer be readily offset by more efficient U.S. production facilities. In today's highly competitive international marketplace, the highest-paid workers also may be the least secure. The same work often can be done at lower pay levels in other countries.

Another reason that unemployment has grown more stubborn involves U.S. demographic trends and the changing composition of the country's labor force. The job market in recent years has had to try to absorb sharp increases in two large segments of the working population—women and teenagers. Increasingly, women who in another era might have been content to remain at home are seeking jobs. Nearly six of every ten married women nowadays work, up from fewer than three in ten in the early postwar years. At the same time, the teenage segment of the population, for various demographic reasons, has swelled greatly over the postwar years. This, too, has caused what amounts to a sharp increase in the need for more jobs.

Minimum-wage regulations and restrictive hiring practices dictated by some unions, tend, of course, to exacerbate this problem. In brief, the growth of the job market—indeed, the growth of the economy—hasn't quite managed to keep abreast of booming demands for jobs.

What has been happening can perhaps best be illustrated by looking again at the coin from the other side. Recent studies show that the percentage of the working-age population with jobs actually increased during recent periods of relatively high unemployment. In 1974, for example, when the unemployment rate rose from about 5 percent of the labor force to more than 7 percent, the percentage of the working-age population *with* jobs rose as well, from about 55 percent to 57 percent—which was a record high for this rarely publicized but significant statistical series. In the mid-1980s, the rate climbed above 60 percent.

Viewed in this way, the problem of unemployment, though undeniably serious and more worrisome than in the early postwar years, seems a good deal less dire than it occasionally is painted by union leaders and some politicians—usually ones heavily obligated to organized labor for its support at election time.

GAUGING THE IMPACT

How has the changing makeup of the economy altered the nature of the business cycle? What is the net effect on the cyclical pattern of such long-term developments as the growing governmental role, the swing to services, the economy's increasing susceptibility to inflation, and the increasing unemployment problem?

Economists hold a wide range of opinions on these concerns. David M. Gordon, an economist at the New School for Social Research in New York, has argued that the U.S. economy is strapped helplessly to a very nasty roller coaster—the business cycle—on a ride made rough by shrinking company profits, worsening unemployment, and unmanageable inflation. In 1975, in a *New York Times Magazine* article titled "Recession Is Capitalism as Usual," Mr. Gordon concludes that "economic stability cannot endure in capitalist countries." Mr. Gordon plainly feels that the economy's cyclical behavior is a deeply worrisome facet of the economic scene, and one that he apparently believes can be eradicated only through a change in the country's economic and political systems, away from free-enterprise capitalism to a centrally run, socialistic arrangement. (A question might be raised in this regard concerning the British experience. That troubled country's economy had been moving sharply leftward in the years before Prime Minister Margaret Thatcher took the helm, but its economic woes eased somewhat thereafter.)

Mr. Gordon's concern over the business cycle—and his eagerness to eliminate it—brings to mind a comment of a very different sort, made years ago by the late Dwight Morrow, perhaps the wisest of the J. P. Morgan partners. "The best way to get rid of business cycles would be to prove they are inevitable," the investment banker remarked. He did not add, though he well might have, that cyclical patterns can be detected in the record of any economic system, including those to the left of Britain and to the right of Uncle Sam.

Friedrich A. von Hayek, the Austrian co-winner of the 1974 Nobel prize in economics, holds a very different view of business-cycle developments from that espoused by Mr. Gordon. "It is not the market economy, or capitalist system, which is responsible" for worsening inflation and unemployment in recent business cycles, the Austrian once declared. "We have in fact been led into a frightful position," he continued. "All politicians promise that they will stop inflation and preserve full employment. But they cannot do this. And the longer they succeed in keeping up employment by continuing inflation, the greater will be the unemployment when the inflation finally comes to an end. There is no magic trick by which we can extricate ourselves from this position which we have created."

Other economists far friendlier to capitalism than David Gordon, however, also express pessimism about the way that they see the business cycle evolving in the United States. William Wolman, an editor of *Business Week* magazine and former

economist of Argus Research Corporation, a New York-based investment-research concern, has warned that "there is a distinct
possibility that the U.S. economy will take on stop-and-go char-
acteristics that have hampered the British economy" in the past.
Another prominent analyst, Albert T. Sommers, chief economist
of New York's Conference Board, worries that "business cycles
have gotten wider and wider." His main fear, he says, "is the
swings may get even wider, and that's something to worry about.
We've got to examine our efforts to stabilize the economy. The
evidence suggests that our failures are getting bigger as time
passes." He adds: "The irony is we thought we had the business
cycle licked."

Perhaps—when the varying arguments have been heard—
the best way to determine how much the nature of the business
cycle has been affected by the long-term trends within the economy is to glance again at those records that have been painstak-
ingly compiled by analysts at the National Bureau of Economic
Research. Since economists at the National Bureau fix precise
dates of cyclical peaks and troughs many months after the
event, records showing the duration of specific expansion and
contraction periods extend only up to the business cycle that began with the upturn of late 1982. Since then, of course, general
economic activity climbed to new highs. The National Bureau
data through 1982, however, are useful in gauging how the cyclical pattern has been changing over the very long run. There are
30 full-fledged business cycles between 1854 and 1982. Solomon
Fabricant's "growth recessions" are not counted. The average
length of the expansion phases, as noted earlier, works out to 33
months and the average length of the contraction phases to 18
months. If the comparable averages only since 1945 are considered, however, the expansions get longer and the recessions
shorter. Between 1945 and 1982 the average length of expansions comes to 45 months and of contractions to 11 months.

The message is that generally, over the long term, expansions have been lengthening and contraction phases have been
getting shorter.

Altogether, the National Bureau records hardly convey the
sort of gloom that comes from such analysts as David Gordon,

or even Albert Sommers. The records indicate, in fact, that the cyclical pattern has gradually grown less volatile—which, after all, is not so remarkable a development in light of the growing importance of the government and of services. As we have seen, the most volatile segment of the economic picture is within manufacturing, where overproduction, inventory misjudgments, and other errors in planning can be large factors. Those appliance dealers at the Merchandise Mart in Chicago—with their perennially mistaken estimates of the business outlook—again come to mind.

Unhappier changes within the economy—inflationary pressures and persistent unemployment—obviously cannot be taken lightly. They unquestionably tend to restrict the strength of expansion phases and make recessions nastier. Ironically, the economy has grown more inflation-prone partly because of the growing governmental role and the swing to services. Ironically, too, unemployment has become stickier partly because a record percentage of the working-age population has endeavored—with unparalleled success—to seek jobs.

The business cycle has been changing, to be sure, and it certainly will continue to change in coming years. But the changes—thus far at least—have not been generally in directions that pessimists stress. The recession-free economy envisaged back in the mid-1960s by Otto Eckstein and others may never materialize. But the evidence indicates that the roller-coaster ride has become—so far at least—less hazardous than it was years ago.

CHAPTER 7

DO-IT-YOURSELF FORECASTING

One may say that the economy is "strong" or "weak." How strong or how weak? We have seen in earlier chapters that this can be gauged with some precision through the use of different statistical yardsticks. These include such headline-grabbing statistics as the unemployment rate, the gross national product, and the consumer-price index, as well as such subtler economic measures as buying power, productivity, and international trade. They all help to define the dimensions—the strength and weakness—of overall economic activity.

In addition, we have seen that by carefully tracking the statistical record it is possible to discern and follow the highly cyclical nature of economic activity, through repeated expansion and contraction phases. We've also seen that it's possible, through a more detailed analysis of the available figures, to detect important changes that occur over many years in the nature of the economy, changes that can influence the economic course without essentially altering its cyclical behavior.

All of this is undeniably important to understanding what is meant by "the economy." But a very large question is left unanswered. The GNP and the unemployment rate, as well as most other yardsticks thus far discussed, tell us a great deal about how the economy looks at a particular moment. But they tell us next to nothing about where the economy may be going. The GNP in a given quarter may amount to such-and-such a figure, up from such-and-such the quarter before. But this does not tell us whether the GNP is likely to move higher still in the coming quarter and the quarter after that.

NO EXPERTISE REQUIRED

Reasonable estimates of the future economic course can be made. And they require remarkably little familiarity with the arcane science of economics.

The importance of such efforts hardly needs elaboration. They are vital, of course, to any investor; clearly, the investment strategy to be followed when good times beckon is not generally the strategy to be followed when a severe recession seems likely.

All sorts of planners, also, depend heavily on the shape of the economic outlook. An automobile producer, for instance, would not want to be caught short of cars if a sharp spurt in economic activity seemed just down the road. By the same token, an official in a policy-making position in Washington would presumably not want to pursue policies likely to retard business activity if a severe contraction seemed imminent.

Once one understands, in general terms, what comprises the economy, a more important, more intriguing game can begin—to try to fathom where the economy will go. This effort, as we will discover, can be undertaken in all sorts of ways. Some are highly unscientific and of questionable validity. Some involve extensive statistical analysis. Some widely followed statistics, that would seem at first glance to be useful indicators of the likely business course, are not. Some yardsticks, less widely known, have served nobly over the years as precursors of general economic activity.

Efforts to forecast the economy's direction, among other things, involve surprises. The unlikeliest matters have turned out to be, for some fortunate individuals, wonderfully prescient indicators of the economic future—"leading" indicators, as they are called in the jargon of economists.

One such individual is Tony Furgueson, a highly successful investment adviser based when I first met him in New York City, just west of Fifth Avenue on 44th Street. The tall, outspoken investment adviser was fortunate, among other reasons, because his office window happened to overlook the windows of a certain hotel of dubious reputation. From his office perch across the street, Mr. Furgueson was able to observe with remarkable clarity, through half-pulled shades in the hotel windows, the level of (for want of a better word) economic activity in the rooms. Over the years, the investment adviser found that the level of this particular activity faithfully foreshadowed major turning points in the overall economy. Business in the rooms, he found, invariably would begin to intensify several months before such broad economic measures as the real GNP and industrial production would begin to turn up from a recession.

Indeed, when I first visited Mr. Furgueson at his 44th Street office in April 1975, his first comment after the handshake was to report most cheerfully that business across the street had recently been showing signs of a pickup—a finding that I quickly confirmed through a glance out the window. At the time, several of the more conventional leading indicators that business forecasters generally follow were still pointing downward—incorrectly, as things turned out.

Mr. Furgueson has not attempted to analyze precisely why the correlation existed between activity across the street and in the overall economy. No doubt a wide range of subtle factors comes into play. For example: was the West 44th Street area of Manhattan favored, for some reason, by visiting salesmen from business concerns in fields that tend to recover faster than most enterprises near the end of recessions? Whatever the explanation, Tony Furgueson was happy to be on 44th Street.

An even stranger leading indicator of economic activity that has proved highly accurate over the years—and doesn't require a perch on 44th Street, or anywhere else in Manhattan for that matter—involves the study of goats. (I kid you not.) An article on the front page of *The Wall Street Journal* in 1975 traced an inverse relationship that has apparently developed through many decades between the trend of the general economy and the country's goat population. When times begin to turn bad, it seems, people breed more goats. In 1973, not long before the 1970 to 1973 economic expansion ended and a recession set in, some 15,000 new purebred goats were registered with the American Dairy Goat Association, located in Spindale, NC. This was nearly three times the number registered in the middle years of the long 1961 to 1969 expansion, when economic activity kept on climbing year after year, from one record to another.

As in the situation at 44th Street, no clear explanation has been given for what *The Wall Street Journal* calls "the goat index." One possibility is that milking a goat can hold down a family's milk bill. On the other hand, goat's milk often costs more at the store—if you can find any—than milk from a cow. The goat indicator remains a puzzle.

The list of unlikely leading indicators of general economic activity extends far beyond goats and goings-on at a particular Manhattan hotel. All sorts of people from time to time have come up with strange ways of divining what lies ahead for the economy. The list includes, for example, the length of women's dresses. When dresses begin to lengthen, the theory holds that economic activity will contract. When hemlines begin to climb, on the other hand, good times supposedly impend.

Again, there is no particular explanation for the relationship—and yet experience unmistakably shows that the relationship does exist. Is it simply that high spirits, in anticipation of better economic times, go with high hemlines, and low spirits, in fear of a recession, go with low hemlines? Or is there a more practical explanation—such as the need of dressmakers to conserve their supplies of material when business appears to be on the rise and to reduce their inventories when they feel that a slump is developing?

Whatever the explanation, the proliferation of pants in recent years renders this indicator less useful than it may once have been for those forecasters bold enough to rely on it.

Nearly as surprising as the reliability of many unlikely leading indicators is the unreliability, as leading indicators, of some exceedingly well known and widely publicized statistics. We have already observed that such broad indexes as the GNP and the unemployment rate tell little about the future direction of business activity. But other yardsticks that one might suppose would help to clarify the crystal balls of economic forecasters generally do not provide any such service.

Automobile statistics are perhaps the outstanding case in

point. Few facets of the economic scene receive more faithful scrutiny in the financial press. This fascination is understandable, to be sure, in an economy as extensively tied to the motor vehicle as ours is. But the record shows, surprisingly, that the much-publicized ups and downs of the automobile business do not necessarily precede or even coincide with the ups and downs of the overall economy.

The record makes this clear. In the six months before the start of the 1960 to 1961 recession, for example, new-car sales soared—from an annual rate of roughly 4 million to a rate of nearly 7 million. Conversely, new-car sales dropped sharply in the six months before the 1960 to 1961 recession ended—and the sales rate continued to decline sharply for another three months after the trough of the recession. A business forecaster who depended on trends in the automobile industry for his prognosticating would have been wrong and wrong again. He would have anticipated further economic expansion just before the 1960 to 1961 recession, and he would have foreseen further months of economic contraction at the very time the economy was beginning to turn up.

"As important as it may be within the broad economic picture, the automobile industry is not a reliable leading indicator of business activity," says Geoffrey Moore of the National Bureau. If the auto industry constitutes any sort of indicator of the economy at all, Mr. Moore says, it would simply be as a "coincident" one—an economic gauge that generally goes up, down, or sideways along with other broad segments of business. The major coincident indicators include, among others, the GNP, the real GNP, and industrial production. These statistical measures are classified by economists as coincident indicators almost by definition. The range of what they encompass is so great that, in fact, they *are* the overall economy.

The automobile business has reached such proportions in the United States that it very nearly falls into the same category. But not quite. The fortunes of the auto industry do not always coincide perfectly with those of business in general. For the economy in general, the 1957 to 1958 recession ended in April 1958. But the auto industry did not begin to turn around until after midyear. As noted, new-car sales continued to fall sharply for several months after the bottom of the 1960 to 1961 recession. Again out of step, the industry kept operating at pre-recession levels for about six months into the 1969 to 1970 economic contraction.

Altogether, the evidence makes clear that the auto industry, however important it may be to the general economic picture, does not serve, for all the attention it receives, as a meaningful indicator of what may lie ahead. Indeed, it does not always reflect even the current condition of business in general. It occasionally will move in one direction and the rest of the economy—in terms of consumer spending, the remaining 90 percent-plus—will move in another direction.

Other economic gauges that receive considerable attention but seem of limited use as leading indicators include most consumer surveys periodically conducted by various economic research organizations. Probably the best known of these is a "survey of consumer attitudes," taken by the University of Michigan's Survey Research Center at Ann Arbor. A typical Michigan survey is based on hour-long personal interviews with 1,406 respondents selected from a nationwide sample of consumers. Conducted regularly since 1951, the Michigan surveys attempt to measure, in the words of the former director, Jay Schmiedeskamp, "consumer expectations and intentions to buy." The interviews, moreover, are designed "to explore reasons for changes in attitudes."

Another widely followed survey is the Conference Board's "consumer confidence index." This survey covers 10,000 households across the country. It focuses particularly on consumer buying plans. For example, it measures the percentage of households polled who plan to buy, say, a new car during the next six months. Such percentages are then compared with the corresponding earlier figures and the "confidence index" is adjusted accordingly.

Not surprisingly, such surveys—and there are more than the two described—tend often to be viewed as harbingers of overall business. Their design certainly suggests that they would tend to signal future economic developments. Yet, strangely, experience shows that such surveys, like the auto industry, generally behave more like coincident, rather than leading, indicators.

This can be seen, among other places, in a perusal of *Business Conditions Digest,* a most useful statistical report published monthly by the Commerce Department. *BCD,* as it is often called, traces the ups and downs of scores of economic statistics in chart form back through most of the period since World War II. Superimposed on the chart lines for each statistical series are shaded areas, representing recession phases of the business cycle. As a result of this method of display, it is a relatively simple matter to glance at the ups and downs of any particular series and determine readily its usual behavior around turning points in the business cycle.

Among the measures recorded in *BCD* is the University of Michigan's survey of consumer attitudes. From its poll, the Survey Research Center has constructed an "index of consumer sentiment," and the movement of this index is shown, through expansion and contraction phases of the general economy, in the Commerce Department publication. A glance at the chart shows, for instance, that the index was still dropping at the trough of the 1969 to 1970 recession and was climbing sharply in the fall of 1973, near the peak of the 1970 to 1973 expansion.

Geoffrey Moore of the National Bureau—the organization that sets the expansion and recession dates used by the Commerce Department for the shaded areas in the *BCD* charts—cautions against using the Michigan or Conference Board surveys, or others like them, as leading indicators.

Many series traced in *BCD* are labeled according to their usual business-cycle timing—leading, coincident, or lagging. The last category, as the label suggests, embraces economic indicators found to move up, down or sideways *after* general economic activity has done so.

Gardner Ackley, an economics professor who chaired the President's Council of Economic Advisers during the mid-1960s, flatly warns executives: "Don't rely too heavily on the consumer sentiment index when making marketing decisions." Geoffrey Moore cautions that the index seems "to be registering, rather than anticipating, what's happening to the rate of change in sales—that is, the rate of change in what people are buying." Mr. Moore's favorite gauge of consumer attitudes, in fact, is not a household survey of any sort. It is a relatively obscure index compiled until recently by the Bureau of Labor Statistics. Called the quit rate, the index shows the number of people who decide to quit their jobs, as a percentage of the number employed.

"It takes a hell of a lot of confidence to quit your job," the National Bureau economist says, adding that "the quit rate is one objective measure of confidence—where somebody has to do something, take some specific action to register his confidence." Unfortunately, the BLS was forced by a tight budget to stop compiling the quit rate in a move that was penny-wise but pound-foolish.

However one may endeavor to judge consumer confidence and subsequent consumer buying intentions, one fact is clear. Anticipating the business cycle, while it may not require economic expertise, does require a familiarity with many statistical yardsticks. One must be aware, for example, that such measures as the unemployment rate and surveys of consumers' plans generally disclose only how things stand at the given moment. In addition, one should be able to recognize those yardsticks—and there are many—that have proved over the years to be reasonably reliable precursors of the economy.

Fortunately for those of us who do not reside on Manhattan's West 44th Street, or have no knowledge of the demographics of goats, there are a considerable number of generally available, bona fide leading indicators. Most are listed, clearly labeled as such, in the pages of *BCD*.

Before taking up individual leading indicators that should be monitored by anyone who wishes to estimate the economy's likely direction, a word or two should be inserted about the origins of the main "leaders," as these indicators are often called.

Before World War I, economists at Harvard University selected several statistical series that seemed promising as economic indicators. These came to be called the Harvard ABC curves. These early yardsticks included the movement of stock prices, the dollar volume of checks drawn on bank deposits, and the rate of interest on short-term business loans. Warren Persons, a Harvard economist, demonstrated that the so-called ABC curves tended to move in definite patterns related to the ups and downs of general business activity. For example, it was observed that stock prices generally tended to move ahead of— to "lead"—the overall economy.

Writing in *Scientific American* in 1975, Geoffrey Moore attempted to explain the basis of the Harvard ABC curves. The three main yardsticks, or curves, he noted, "typically moved in sequence: stock prices first, bank debits next, and interest rates last." Mr. Moore went on to explain: "The economic logic of the sequence was that tight money and high interest rates led to a decline in business prospects and a drop in stock prices, which led to cutbacks in investment and a recession in business. The recession, in turn, led to easier money and lower interest rates, which eventually improved business prospects, lifted stock prices, and generated a new expansion of economic activity."

The Harvard economists managed to construct, using this small assortment of indicators, highly cyclical patterns of statistics. Each yardstick moved up and down like the overall economy, but not necessarily at the same time as the economy.

The ABC curves fell into disuse after 1929, in part because they failed to flash a warning about the severe economic contraction that developed late that year. One reason for this failure was that stock prices, viewed as a leading indicator among the curves, behaved instead like a coincident indicator. Stock prices turned down with, rather than ahead of, general business activity. Since then, stock prices have almost unfailingly led the economy and are once again highly regarded as a harbinger of overall business. Analysts believe that their failure to perform as a leading indicator in 1929 may have stemmed from the severity of that stock-market plunge, one of the sharpest on record. It was so sharp that, rather than signaling deep trouble ahead for the economy, it had a direct, immediate impact, actually *causing* deep trouble by wiping out savings and destroying the buying power and confidence of families at virtually all economic levels.

During the 1930s, various economists continued trying to refine the art of forecasting through the use of statistical indicators. Extensive research was undertaken at the National Bureau in New York. Its economists studied the cyclical behavior of dozens of statistics. In late 1937, Henry Morgenthau, Jr., President Franklin D. Roosevelt's Secretary of the Treasury, asked the nonprofit research organization to devise for the government a standardized set of indicators that would help Washington's policymakers ascertain more accurately where the economy seemed headed. The request grew out of a deep frustration at the White House over the fact that the economy, after finally pulling out of the disastrous 1929 to 1933 contraction phase and staging a recovery, once again was beginning to nose downward.

Under the direction of Wesley C. Mitchell, aided by Arthur Burns, later to become chairman of the Federal Reserve Board, the National Bureau late in 1937 gave Mr. Morgenthau an approved list of indicators. It included not only leading indicators but coincident and lagging indicators as well. Used in tandem, the last two categories are also of value in forecasting the business course. The National Bureau list was first published, with Washington's seal of approval, in May 1938.

In the half century since then, the list was revised six times—in 1950, 1960, 1966, 1975, 1979 and 1983. The revisions were made each time to take into account new statistics, made available by more extensive surveys and by the use of computers in compiling statistical material. The revisions also reflected periodic efforts to allow for important changes in the makeup of the economy, such as those discussed in Chapter Six. The revision in 1975, for example, attempted to allow more fully for the economy's increasing susceptibility to inflation. It was found in late 1973, just before the recession began, that many leading indicators, which should have been flashing red and dropping, instead were climbing, falsely suggesting fair economic weather ahead. The indicators involved mainly were denominated in dollars—not in so-called constant dollars, which go into the real GNP, but in unadjusted "current" dollars, the kind in our wallets that are eroded by inflation.

The 1975 revision of the indicators attempted, among other things, to remove some—but not all—statistical series that can be pushed up simply by rising prices. Not surprisingly, indicators that have survived through the various revisions since 1937 tend to be ones not expressed in simple dollar terms. An example is the length of the average workweek in industry. When it gets longer, this suggests a rising level of business activity several months down the road. When it shortens, declining economic activity is indicated.

Presently, we will take up in detail the key indicators. For the moment, suffice it to say that analysts have broadly segregated the many statistical series that appear in *BCD* into a few major categories—those involving jobs, those related to production, those involving investment and inventories, those concerned with prices, costs, and profits, and those involving that most basic of economic matters—money. Because money is such an important precursor of general economic developments, and also is so often misunderstood, it is well worth our while to take a close look at this particular leading indicator.

MONEY

Money is the change in your pocket. But it takes other forms as well. Some are readily recognizable, others are not.

Money, essentially, is a tool. It serves a function—to facilitate exchanges of goods and services. Any medium of exchange that provides this function, in effect, is money. Through the ages, all sorts of items, not normally thought of as such, have served as money. The list ranges from stones, used in some primitive societies, to cigarettes, used in war-ravaged countries in supposedly sophisticated modern times.

Gold, particularly, has been used through the centuries as money, though it does not serve—officially at least—as money in the United States today. The yellow metal constitutes a highly tangible medium of exchange, and it possesses other important monetary qualities. The value of a piece of gold varies, of course, according to its size and purity. Because it can be so precisely valued, gold can serve also as a standard of exchange. In a particular business transaction, the amount and quality of gold involved can be tailored exactly to the importance of the transaction. In addition, because it is one of the most enduring products known, it can serve as a store of value. It does not fade or erode over the years. Paper money, obviously, boasts no such qualities. Moreover, the long-term value of paper money can easily diminish—as a result of the basic forces of supply and demand—if too much of it is printed. This has not been a problem with gold, which must be laboriously dug out of the ground and refined at great expense.

Today, in the United States, two kinds of money are predominantly used. The first we have noted—the coins and paper bills in the pockets and purses of the public. The second kind of money, which is far more significant, is that held in checking and savings accounts in commercial banks and other such institutions. Economists call the checking-account form of money "demand deposits." They are, as the name implies, deposits that must be paid on the demand of depositors. We know this form of money as, simply, our checking accounts.

When economists talk—or more likely argue with one another—about the role of "money" in the economy, they normally are talking about —at the least—two forms of money: currency in the pockets of the public and demand deposits. Together, these two forms of money comprise what economists in their textbooks call M-1. Demand deposits comprise more than three quarters of M-1. When we read in newspapers that the nation's money supply during a particular week or month or quarter or year grew at such-and-such a percentage, the money supply in question usually is M-1.

Anyone attempting to anticipate the general course of the economy should try to keep abreast of M-1. This involves not only keeping a tab on the pertinent statistics, which are issued weekly by the Federal Reserve and show precisely where M-1 stands each week. It also necessitates a familiarity with ways in which the movement of M-1 can be anticipated. And this requires a brief discussion of how money—that is, M-1—is created in the United States.

First, however, it should be observed that M-1 is by no means the only way that economists define the nation's money supply. Besides M-1, there are M-2 and M-3. Without going into elaborate detail, suffice it to say that, generally, the higher the number of the particular "M," the more comprehensive it is.

As we have seen, M-1 comprises currency and demand deposits. M-2 embraces these two categories, plus smaller-sized time deposits, which are, simply, savings-type deposits of less than $100,000 left with thrift institutions over periods of time. Like demand deposits, as a rule they bear interest. Broader is M-3, which includes all of M-2 plus large-denomination time deposits. And larger still is L, or M-3 plus nonbank holdings of Treasury bills, commercial paper, and the like.

To anticipate the movement of general business activity, it is important to follow the movement, at the least, of M-1. Experience shows that the overall economy tends to follow the path of the money supply, with a lag of several months or more. The Federal Reserve reports M-1's exact total and recent movement normally every Thursday afternoon. The details appear Fridays in such newspapers as *The Wall Street Journal* and *The New York Times*. A supplementary statistical report on monetary developments is issued weekly by the Federal Reserve System's regional bank in St. Louis, one of a dozen such regional outposts of the Washington-based central-bank system. The St. Louis Federal Reserve Bank will mail its report, which contains elaborate analytic detail about monetary trends, to individuals who wish to receive it.

It also is possible to gain valuable insights into the likely movement of the money supply. This requires an understanding of how money is created in the United States. That process is supervised by the Federal Reserve Board in Washington and the so-called Federal Open Market Committee. The Federal Reserve Board is made up of seven governors, as noted earlier, each appointed by the President for 14-year terms. The Federal Open Market Committee is composed of the seven governors of the Reserve Board, plus five presidents of regional Federal Reserve banks. The FOMC, as it is commonly known, meets in Washington at the Federal Reserve Building on Constitution Avenue, which also houses the Reserve Board, its seven governors, and a large staff of economists and statisticians.

The Federal Reserve System, through the Reserve Board and the FOMC, controls the country's money supply mainly in three ways. The Reserve Board sets the level of so-called reserve requirements that banks must keep on hand, rather than lend. The banks are required by the Board to keep on hand, in the form of cash, a specified percentage of their demand deposits.

This has the effect of limiting the amount of lending that banks can safely undertake. The higher the level of reserve requirements, the more restricted becomes bank lending.

When banks lend, this tends to expand the nation's money supply, through what economists call a "multiplier" effect. As money is lent, deposited in other banks, and lent again—and as this process is repeated again and again—the demand-deposit component of the money supply obviously will rise sharply. It is possible, through mathematics, to determine the theoretical limit of this multiplier effect. The particular limit will depend on where the Reserve Board sets the percentage for reserves required to be set aside. If banks are instructed, for example, to maintain cash reserves of 15 percent against their demand deposits, the theoretical limit of the multiplier effect for an original $1,000 demand deposit works out to $6,667. This happens because diminishing fractions of the original $1,000 are lent and re-lent through the banking system. This arrangement is called a *fractional-reserve* type of banking system.

No such multiplier process, it should be noted, applies to currency in circulation, the other component of M-1. Accordingly, an increase in the currency component of M-1 normally will have less economic impact than an increase in the demand-deposit component, where the multiplier effect is involved.

Monetary expansion is also controlled through what is called the discount rate. When they need funds for loans or other purposes, private banks, as members of the Federal Reserve System, may borrow from regional Federal Reserve banks. The discount rate is the interest charged by the regional banks on such loans. Like an increase in reserve requirements, an increase in the discount rate tends eventually to restrict monetary expansion. Conversely, a reduction in the discount rate, like a reduction in reserve requirements, tends to foster growth of the money supply.

The third major way in which the money supply is controlled involves the Federal Open Market Committee. The FOMC meets in Washington once or twice a month. At the start of each meeting, Federal Reserve economists give the FOMC a report on economic conditions in the country and abroad, as the Fed analysts picture the situation. Later in the meeting, the 12

FOMC members vote on what sort of monetary policy should be pursued until the next meeting. The FOMC issues a "directive" that is given to an official of the Federal Reserve System's main regional bank in New York City. This official is the manager of operations of the New York Fed's so-called Open Market Account. In accordance with his instructions from the FOMC, he attempts to direct the operations of the Open Market Account in such a way as to carry out as nearly as possible the particular monetary policy sought by the FOMC.

Through the New York bank's Open Market Account, the manager is empowered to buy or sell, for the Federal Reserve System, government securities in dealings with private concerns that make a market in such issues. If the FOMC has directed him, for example, to manage the Open Market Account with an eye to fostering a more expansionary monetary policy, he will normally order increased purchases of securities by the Open Market Account. This buying tends to pump money from the Federal Reserve System into the private economy, as the New York Fed pays private sellers for securities it buys. Conversely, when a more restrictive monetary policy is desired, the Open Market Account normally moves to sell government securities. This tends to pull money out of the private economy into Federal Reserve coffers.

Many economists feel that this third method of regulating monetary growth is far and away the most potent means available to policymakers. A 47-page booklet called "Open Market Operations," published by the New York Federal Reserve Bank, explains that when the Federal Reserve, for instance, "buys securities in the open market, it creates bank reserves which did not exist before." The Fed makes payments simply by crediting the amount of its purchase to the account of the particular commercial bank involved in the transaction. As a result, money is created. The booklet goes on to note that this money-creating power derives from the Congress, which is given the authority under the U.S. Constitution (Article I, Section 8) to "coin money [and] regulate the value thereof."

It is a simple matter to pinpoint this money-creating process by the Federal Reserve. Near the end of 1987, for example, Fed reports show that M-1 totaled about $761 billion. The bulk of that—roughly $500 billion—was made up by demand deposits, with currency in circulation accounting for much of the rest. At the same time, M-2 amounted to about $2.9 trillion. The far larger total, of course, reflects the inclusion of time deposits. M-3 totaled $3.7 trillion.

Over the years, as a result of Federal Reserve policies—intentional and otherwise—M-1 has grown unevenly. In the decade to mid-1965, a period that covers two recessions, M-1 grew at an average yearly rate of 2.2 percent. In the next decade, this growth accelerated to more than 5 percent yearly.

There is considerable debate among economists over just how fast the money supply should grow. A large group, led by Milton Friedman of the University of Chicago, has long argued that the monetary growth rate should be consistent with the economy's own, natural ability to grow—in effect, the rate at which the real GNP can be expected to expand in accordance with the country's resources of labor, material, and technical know-how. A figure often mentioned by Mr. Friedman and others is roughly 3 percent annually. If the growth of M-1 exceeds that level over prolonged periods, as it has done in many recent years, this will act to push the economy forward too strongly and drive up prices, Friedmanite economists contend. They blame much of the inflation and subsequent economic stagnation in recent decades—the term often applied is "stagflation"—on excessive monetary expansion.

On the other hand, these same analysts warn that monetary growth considerably below the 3 percent level over prolonged periods, or actual reductions in the money supply, will tend to restrict economic activity severely and eventually bring on widespread price-cutting. This is precisely what happened, Friedmanites claim, between 1929 and 1933, a period in which the money supply contracted by about a third. A far different, expansionary monetary policy, they argue, would have largely prevented the severity of the economic contraction that developed. These economists, who obviously lay great emphasis on the importance of monetary policy within the overall economic picture, also stress that the Federal Reserve should avoid sharp monetary swings—swings from very high rates of monetary growth to actual shrinkages of the money supply. Such a roller-coaster policy, it is argued, serves only to make the economy's already cyclical behavior more pronounced and more hazardous.

In fact, possibly because the Friedmanite advice is difficult for policymakers to follow for a variety of practical reasons, monetary growth has been anything but moderate and steady. And, however annoying this unevenness may be to Mr. Friedman and his disciples, it does provide an important forecasting tool for anyone trying to figure out the future course of the economy.

One place where monetary developments can be readily followed—somewhat more leisurely than by scrutinizing the weekly reports of the Federal Reserve—is in the Commerce Department's monthly publication *Business Conditions Digest.* Among leading indicators listed there are several gauges of the money supply. These include changes in M-1 and M-2. The indicators take the form of percentage changes occurring monthly in the various categories of money.

A glance at the pertinent charts in *BCD* shows that over the years these monetary indicators have correctly, promptly signaled major turning points in the overall economy. The chart for M-2, for example, shows that this particular leading indicator, adjusted for inflation, has correctly foreshadowed every major recession and every expansion phase of the economy in the last 25 years—which is about as far back as the chart goes. Not only that: The record shows that the M-2 indicator has done so earlier than most other leading indicators.

A parenthetical footnote should be inserted here, to underline the value of the money supply as a precursor of economic movement. The 1929 to 1933 economic contraction came as a great surprise and shock to most forecasters. As noted, the stock market, a leading indicator, for once gave no warning. However, anyone following money-supply trends—had that been possible then—would have begun growing cautious about the economic outlook as far back as 1928, when monetary expansion started to flatten out. Unfortunately, regular reports providing detailed monetary statistics were not available in 1928 and 1929. The statistics, which we have in considerable detail for those years now, showing the contraction of the money supply in 1929 to

1933, have been reconstructed largely by Milton Friedman and Anna Schwartz, a National Bureau economist, through a painstaking perusal of old bank records and other such data.

Mention also should be made of the problem that inflation poses for anyone attempting to gauge the economic outlook solely by the movement, say, of M-1. Rising prices tend to diminish the amount of stimulation that a given increase in the money supply will impart to the economy. If prices rise 10 percent and the money supply also rises 10 percent, "real" monetary expansion, in the jargon of economists, is reduced to zero. In such circumstances, a 10 percent increase in the money supply would actually be less indicative of future growth in business activity than, for instance, a 5 percent money-supply increase at a time when prices are rising only 2 percent. In the latter situation, real money-supply growth amounts to 3 percent.

In recent years, it has become increasingly necessary to take developments on the price front into account when one examines monetary indicators. To illustrate: The rate of growth in M-1 began to slow in late 1972, about a year before the advent of the severe 1973 to 1975 recession. However, M-1 did continue to expand before the recession hit in late 1973. That growth, viewed in isolation, without regard to the price picture, gave scant indication of the severity of the recession to come.

The 1972 to 1973 behavior of M-1 was in contrast to its behavior before recessions earlier in the post–World War II era, when inflation was not a major economic worry. For several months before the 1960 to 1961 recession, for instance, M-1 actually declined. No such decline was evident in 1972 to 1973. However, in real terms, allowing for rising prices, the money supply indeed did decline before and during much of the 1973 to 1975 recession. The forecaster who viewed M-1 in these terms during 1972 to 1973 would have had a much clearer warning of the approach and magnitude of the recession than persons who monitored only M-1, without taking the steep price increases into account.

There are extreme circumstances, to be sure, when following real money-supply trends can be misleading. One occurred during the Great Depression. As mentioned, the money supply shrank sharply between 1929 and 1933. But the economic contraction itself was so severe that prices collapsed along with the money supply. In fact, prices for a while fell even faster than the money supply. An economist visiting from Mars, examining the money-supply statistics in real terms, would have seen a moderate rise in the figures. And, from this, he might reasonably have concluded that a period of rising economic activity was unfolding. He would, of course, have been dead wrong. A disastrous decline in economic activity was in fact under way.

Nonetheless, under normal circumstances, the trend of the money supply, expressed in real terms after adjustment for price changes, constitutes a most important leading indicator. Indeed, its importance has recently become more widely recognized. The 1975 changes in the key leading indicators contained in *BCD* include the introduction of a new statistical series—the money supply expressed in terms of the buying power of the dollar for a particular year.

The decisions reached at FOMC meetings are not made public until many weeks afterward. This secrecy, policymakers claim, is necessary to prevent. among other things, private speculators from possibly profiting in transactions involving securities traded by the New York Fed's Open Market Account. Some critics of the Federal Reserve contend that this secrecy on the part of the FOMC is unwarranted. Whether it is or not, there are other ways to anticipate money-supply trends besides trying to develop a pipeline into the deliberations of the FOMC. One way is simply to observe the actions of the New York Fed. These are publicly reported weekly, along with the money-supply statistics, usually on Thursday afternoons. The reports show, along with other such activities, Federal Reserve purchases or sales of government securities during the preceding week. These figures can provide an idea of Federal Reserve intentions, regardless of what may actually have happened to the money supply itself during the week.

Such weekly data, however, can prove confusing. Due to special factors that often arise, the long-run intentions of the FOMC tend to be obscured in the weekly statistics. Anyone depending too heavily on such reports from week to week runs the same sort of risk as the proverbial fellow who fails to see the forest because he has been too busy concentrating on the trees.

A better way to anticipate monetary trends is to try to analyze the sort of thinking likely to prevail among monetary policymakers at a given time. This is not as difficult an undertaking
as it may at first glance appear. The ability to mind-read is decidedly not a requirement.

Few policymakers would argue strongly with Mr. Friedman's idea that in the Unites States, over the long run, M-1
should rise at an annual rate of about 3 percent, approximately
in line with the economy's ability to grow. In practice, however,
policymakers rarely seem free to get down seriously to the business of gearing money-supply growth to the prescribed long-run
rate. Rather, they invariably become preoccupied with immediate concerns, such as whether the money supply appears ade-
quate to prevent a spiraling of interest rates, or whether it is
growing sufficiently to enable the overall economy to pull out of
a recession, or, at the other extreme, whether it is growing
slowly enough to prevent overstimulation and inflationary
strains during an expansionary phase of the business cycle.

Further complicating the task of the money-supply managers is something that Mr. Friedman, in his call for steady,
moderate monetary growth over the years, may tend to overlook—the huge budget deficits so frequently run up by elected
politicians, in Congress and in the White house, who understandably find spending money far easier than raising it from
taxpayers, who also happen to be voters.

Budget deficits occur, of course, when the federal government spends more than it takes in. This process naturally acts
to drive up interest rates. The government—specifically, the
Treasury Department—is normally compelled to borrow funds
in order to make up the financial shortage.

This borrowing can occur in different ways. The Treasury
can compete for money in the so-called open market, attempting
to divert investors' funds that might otherwise be lent, say, to a
private corporation also in need of money. This competition naturally tends to force up interest rates. More borrowers compete
for funds in the marketplace, and in the process interest rates
begin to climb.

However, the Federal Reserve also can purchase government securities, as we have seen. The money managers at the
Fed may fear that the Treasury's borrowing needs are of such

magnitude at a particular time that interest rates in the open market may climb too sharply for the general health of business. The Fed officials, in such circumstances, could decide to buy some or all of the securities that the Treasury is attempting to sell to raise money to meet the budget deficit.

The phrase that economists apply to this process is "monetizing the debt." It is an appropriate description. The upshot of such action is to create new money in the economy. The procedure may relieve interest-rate pressures for the moment. But in the longer run, such pressures may develop anyway—because increases in the money supply ultimately serve to push up interest rates. This is because excessive money-supply increases lead eventually to higher prices, and if lenders fear rising prices, they will logically seek higher rates of interest on what they lend, in order to protect the long-term value of their loans.

Such considerations, however, are unlikely to take precedence, in the deliberations of monetary policymakers, over considerations that involve the immediate health of the economy. Time and again, the exigencies of the current economic situation have proved decisive in policy moves. This attitude may be unfortunate for the long-term health of the economy. But it enables observers far removed from the Washington scene to estimate the likely monetary course to be pursued at a particular moment. One may simply examine the economic situation confronting, say, the FOMC before one of its meetings and then deduce the probable way in which the policymakers will react to it.

Some general assumptions can be made, and one certainly need not be a financial expert to make them. If a large deficit looms in the federal budget at a time when interest rates generally are at high levels—above 12 percent, for example, on the bonds of the best-known, most prestigious corporations—the likelihood is that monetary authorities will provide any needed assistance to the Treasury in financing the budget debt. And, as a result, the money supply is likely to expand substantially.

On the other hand, if the federal budget is approximately in balance or in surplus—a rarity in recent decades—there will be no particular need, as economists put it, to monetize the debt. Policymakers will more likely pursue only moderate monetary expansion, in line with the long-term growth potential of the economy.

Another important consideration is the amount of inflation in the economy. If inflation is nonexistent or mild—again, rare nowadays—policymakers will doubtless feel freer to pursue monetary expansion than if inflation is a severe, worsening problem.

It's worth noting that a dilemma can develop for the authorities when the desire to prevent an interest-rate spiral in the short run runs into the desire to curb inflation. In the long run, as explained, high interest rates go hand in hand with high rates of price increase. In recent years, the dilemma has usually been resolved so as to prevent spiraling interest rates in the short run. As interest rates rise and funds become more and more difficult for borrowers to obtain, a point is reached where concern develops at the Federal Reserve over the financial viability of beleaguered borrowers. Whenever this point approaches, the money managers—ever mindful of the disastrous experience of 1929 to 1933—invariably seem to relent in their long-term inflation-fighting and open the monetary spigot to prevent spreading bankruptcies in the short run. Despite persistent inflation, for example, the Federal Reserve eased monetary policy dramatically after the Penn Central became strapped in 1970, and took similar action after the Franklin National Bank ran into financial trouble in 1974.

A final point should be made about the behavior of the monetary authorities. As the 1973 to 1975 recession showed, they tend not to be especially sensitive to unemployment figures. Monetary policy, which had been growing more restrictive in a battle against worsening inflation, did not clearly begin to ease until late in 1974. By then, the jobless rate had been rising for about a year. This seeming indifference to unemployment no doubt reflects the fact that, unlike Congressmen, and the President who appoints them to their 14-year-terms, the Fed governors are not elected officials. To some degree, therefore, they are insulated from attack by, say, angry labor leaders. At the same time, however, as managers of the country's money and banking system, they do exhibit considerable concern, as we have seen, if trouble brews on the financial front.

It is possible, then, to gauge with reasonable precision the way in which the monetary authorities are likely at a given time to decide policy. Prevailing economic conditions will almost certainly determine whether a speedup in the growth of the money supply is likely, or perhaps a slowdown, or perhaps simply a continuation of existing policy.

A word of warning is necessary here. Monetary officials are not always able to produce precisely the results they deem most suitable. It is possible, for example, that the FOMC may order the New York Fed to conduct its open-market securities operations in such a way as to step up the growth of M-1 from, say, 2 percent annually to 7 percent annually. Through the procedures previously discussed, new money can be pumped into the banking system, through newly created demand deposits at commercial banks. However, it is possible that business demand for loans may prove to be lagging—that the new money will not be lent and re-lent as swiftly as the authorities might have anticipated. This could tend to hold actual expansion of the demand-deposit component of M-1 far below the potential, desired growth theoretically possible through the aforementioned multiplier phenomenon. In such a situation, economists would say that the *velocity*—or rate of turnover—of the money supply is lagging.

Some economists—mainly those associated with the views of Milton Friedman—believe that the Federal Reserve, if it makes the proper effort, can indeed control the growth of the money supply with great accuracy. But other economists—especially many who profess to emphasize the ideas of the British economist John Maynard Keynes—question whether monetary officials can in fact control money-supply growth with such precision. Indeed, many Keynesian-school economists question the entire Friedmanite notion that the trend of the money supply is central to the general condition of the economy. The Keynesians stress the importance of governmental spending and taxing— rather than monetary policy—in determining economic developments.

The questioning of the Federal Reserve's ability to exercise exact control over the expansion of the money supply undoubtedly contains some validity. But the record gives scant support to any argument that the course of money supply and the course of the overall economy are unrelated. Not only are the two clearly intertwined but they are intertwined in such a way that money-supply trends foreshadow—by at least several months, and often longer—trends in overall business.

STOCKS

When economists of the Commerce Department and the National Bureau worked to revise and improve the list of leading indicators in 1975, in the process they assigned a rating to each indicator, much as a teacher assigns a mark between 100 and zero to student. Considerations used to determine each indicator's mark included such factors as timing, economic significance, and prompt availability. The 12 leading indicators were assigned marks ranging from a low of 69 to a top mark of 80. The bottom grade went to a relatively obscure yardstick titled, mysteriously, "vendor performance." Briefly, it measures the speed with which goods are delivered to customers. The index keeps track of the percentage of companies reporting slower deliveries each month. A rising percentage signifies a future rise in overall economic activity, and a drop in the percentage suggests a coming economic slowdown.

A monetary yardstick on the list of 12, reflecting monthly changes in M-1, fared better, receiving a mark of 79. It was judged to provide especially early signals of future changes in the economic direction. The M-1 yardstick was found to have foreshadowed recessions by 10 months and recovery periods by 8 months.

The indicator that achieved the top mark of 80 is far less obscure than the vendor-performance measure and far less complicated than the money-supply gauges. The top mark went to the stock market. The precise measure of share prices used is a broad index compiled by Standard & Poor's Corporation. It measures overall changes in the prices of 500 major common stocks. The more widely publicized and older stock-market index. The Dow Jones industrial average, is not listed among the key leading indicators contained in *Business Conditions Digest* because it is based on only 30 stocks. Over the years, however, its movement has closely paralleled that of Standard & Poor's index of 500 stocks.

The stock market is by no means new to the list of key leading indicators. It has survived through the various revisions of the leading-indicator list back to 1937 because, again and again, it has provided early notice of coming changes in overall economic activity. On the average, it has turned down eight months before recession periods set in and turned up four months before economic recoveries. The money supply—the version now used is M-2, adjusted for inflation—has usually given slightly longer signals, but no leading indicator, the money-supply gauges included, is so promptly available. Indeed, if one chooses to follow the actual stock-market tape that emanates from the floor of the New York Stock Exchange, with its ticker symbols and price information, changes in individual share prices may be scrutinized on a minute-by-minute basis.

The high standing of the stock market as a leading economic indicator may seem surprising to many readers. A volatile economic measure, the stock market has occasionally been ridiculed as a misleading—rather than a leading—indicator. Prominent among its critics is M.I.T.'s Paul Samuelson, who has commented that "the stock market has correctly predicted nine out of the last five recessions."

Julius Shiskin of the Bureau of Labor Statistics, an authority (along with Geoffrey Moore of the National Bureau) on the subject of leading indicators, sharply disagreed with such criticism: "Despite some support for Professor Samuelson's apparent view that the market is nothing but a collection of random events—a view held by many on Wall Street—I believe the evidence to the contrary is persuasive." The Standard & Poor's stock index, Mr. Shiskin went on, "is one of the best-known and most valuable of all economic indicators; investors use it to form first impressions of the tide of their own market activities and business economists use it widely as an indicator of prospective business-cycle developments." A similar view comes from Albert Cox of Lionel Edie. "Stock prices have proven to be a highly accurate leading indicator of the business cycle over more than 100 years of recorded experience," the economist declares.

Underlying the stock market's outstanding performance as an indicator of the future course of the economy is its complex relationship to other facets of the economic scene. One such link is its relationship to the profits of the corporation whose shares are constantly being traded by investors. Mr. Shiskin explained this relationship this way: "Say that it becomes known that a company is likely to earn less or perhaps lose money in the quarters ahead. Many people will offer the stock for sale, and the market price for that stock is likely to decline. The declines will tend to be spread . . . as the prospects [for reduced earnings] for various companies become known. Both an interaction and a cumulative downward effect on the stock price index is likely to take place. The decline in aggregate profits can be expected to result in a decline in new investment and still later in a decline in production and employment."

The main reason that corporate profits themselves are no longer among the key leading indicators listed in *Business Conditions Digest*—they were removed during the 1975 revision—is that, unlike the stock market, profit figures are exceedingly slow to be published. They are compiled quarterly, rather than monthly, and by the time the Commerce Department comes up with the totals each quarter, any change in the economy that may have been signaled may already be under way. Also, of course, they are dollar-denominated and therefore easily distorted by inflation.

Another relationship that no doubt underlies the stock market's ability to presage economic developments so well involves interest rates. Securities that offer fixed rates of interest compete for investors' dollars with common stocks, which offer dividends that may be increased or reduced according to changes in a company's profitability and other corporate developments. When interest rates rise, as they are apt to do when business activity begins to expand too rapidly and generates increased inflationary pressures, such interest-paying securities as corporate bonds tend naturally to become more attractive to investors. Accordingly, money is more likely to flow into the bond market than into the stock market. Conversely, when a recession approaches bottom, demand for loans usually tumbles. This decline in loan demand tends to reduce interest rates and renders interest-paying securities less attractive. In the process, the stock market becomes more enticing to investors.

A 1975 study by Argus Research Corporation, the New York

investment advisory service, examined the remarkable performance of the stock market as a precursor of economic recoveries.
Titled "The Market As a Barometer," the Argus study concluded
that the market's ability to foreshadow an economic upturn "is
not the result of investor clairvoyance." Rather, the report goes
on, "it occurs in response to easing financial conditions which,
in turn, are largely responsible for the recovery that subsequently ensues."

The day-to-day behavior of the stock market, to be sure, is
not entirely rooted in such fundamental factors as interest-rate
and profit trends. Geoffrey Moore of the National Bureau ob-
serves that "a wide variety of factors play upon the market—
shifts in investor confidence, fears of inflation, prospects for
higher taxes or stiffer government regulation, changes in mar-
gin requirements [which limit the amounts that investors may
borrow to buy stocks], the flow of funds from abroad, a strike in
a major industry, the failure of a large enterprise." Such factors,
Mr. Moore believes, "make the underlying regularities [in the
movement of the stock market] more difficult to observe and predict." Indeed, Mr. Samuelson's criticism that the stock market
has forecast nine of the last five recessions is not without a mod-
icum of justification. The Standard & Poor's stock index, as well
as other such indexes, has occasionally dropped sharply during
periods of prolonged economic expansion, before resuming a
long-term climb.

Before moving along to some other important leading indicators, it should perhaps be noted also that an investor who ap-
preciates the stock market's close relationship with the ups and
downs of the business cycle can profit greatly by this understanding. The stock market, as we have seen, can tell us the
likely future direction of business. Using the same sort of analysis, it is possible to gauge the likely direction of the stock market. If one is able to ascertain with reasonable certainty the
probable direction of the economy, one can make some guesses
about the likely direction of the stock market. For example, if
other leading indicators, such as the money supply, strongly suggest that a recession lies six months or so down the road, it is a

fair guess that share prices will be moving progressively lower, if indeed a decline has not already set in. On the other hand, a general rise in key leading indicators during a recession should suggest to investors that a long-term stock-market rise is on the way.

A study by Raymond DeVoe, the stock broker, issued on March 31, 1975, provided an instance in which attention should have been paid to the stock market's relationship to the business cycle—but, unfortunately, was not. Mr. DeVoe likened his feeling about stock-market prospects at that time to the instinctive feeling that skin divers occasionally experience when a large shark is nearby. There is an ominous stillness in the water. The clear message of his analysis was for investors to be wary of the stock market and be ready, in effect, to get out of the water fast.

At the time that the analysis appeared, the Dow Jones industrial average stood at about 750. A month later, the average was above the 800 mark, and within six weeks of Mr. DeVoe's warning it crossed the 850 level. Investors who depended on their instincts on March 31 may or may not have succeeded in catching the sharp rise in share prices. It would depend whether their intuition agreed with Mr. DeVoe's that a large shark was nearby. However, investors wise enough to keep their focus firmly on such key leading indicators as the money supply and building permits for new private housing units, another of those listed in *Business Conditions Digest,* would more than likely have shaken off any instinctive fears about sharks in the water. Those leading indicators, as well as others, had been on the rise since the start of the year.

It should be added that the gains to be made in the stock market during recessions, just before the overall economy has begun to expand, can be enormous—and the economy most certainly was in a recession in March 1975. In the final five months of the 1969 to 1970 recession, the Dow Jones average jumped 25.8 percent. In the first 12 months of the subsequent 1970 to 1973 economic expansion, by comparison, the stock average rose only 4.6 percent. Similarly, in the last four months of the 1960 to 1961 recession, the stock index rose 16.9 percent, while in the next 12 months, when business activity was expanding, the average rose only 6.1 percent. A most dramatic rise in share prices during a postwar recession occurred in the last five months of the 1953 to 1954 slump. The Dow Jones average climbed 37.1 percent during that short period. The increase in the next 12 months, though a substantial 33.6 percent, still fell short of the rise during the recession.

The message that emerges, clearly, is that the investor who waits until a recession is safely over before jumping into the stock market, while he may not miss the boat entirely, certainly misses the chance for a cabin in the first-class section.

THE BIG PICTURE

Anyone attempting to estimate the likely direction of overall business activity, quite obviously, can learn a lot simply by keeping abreast of money-supply trends and stock-market figures. Indeed, there is a temptation here to advise readers to remain glued to the ups and downs of those two leading indicators—and do no more. There is even a temptation to say that the stock market alone—easy to follow, widely publicized, and remarkably accurate in its foreshadowing of business-cycle changes—can signal the likely economic course sufficiently well to enable anyone's crystal ball to function clearly.

The temptation should be resisted. "Why do we need other leading indicators? Why isn't the index of stock prices enough?" Mr. Shiskin of the Bureau of Labor Statistics once asked. He answered his own question: "Experience has taught us that there is no single, fully reliable leading indicator, and that an average of many—such as the index of leading indicators—is better than one." He cited an instance, noted earlier, of the danger involved in depending on just one or two leading indicators. The stock market failed utterly to give early notice of a major change in the direction of the business cycle in 1929. Share prices continued merrily upward in 1929—all the way into the teeth of what turned out to be the severest economic slump in the country's history.

The money supply, like the stock market, occasionally fails as a leading indicator. In addition, the Federal Reserve is in the habit of revising its monetary statistics months after they are originally reported. As a result of such tardy revisions, the monetary picture can suddenly assume a very different shape from what is first seemed. What appears to be a period of rapid growth in the money supply, for example, can turn out, after the Fed makes a revision or two in its statistics, to be only a tiny uptick, or possibly even a time of monetary contraction.

The wisest procedure, accordingly, is to follow—if not religiously every month, at least with reasonable regularity—a limited selection of other leading indicators that have also proved exceptionally reliable over the years.

Considerable attention should be paid to the Commerce Department's composite index of 12 leading indicators. The 12 are selected from many dozens followed by National Bureau analysts. As noted, the makeup of the composite index has been changed repeatedly in a long sequence of attempts to improve its usefulness.

The index has turned down, on the average, some eight months before recession periods and turned up some four months ahead of the start of expansion phases. The component indicators include, as mentioned, the stock market, the M-2 monetary measure, and the vendor-performance yardstick. The other leading indicators deemed by Commerce Department and National Bureau analysts worthy of the select list cover a diverse range. All are available monthly in *Business Conditions Digest.*

The remaining nine include the length of the average workweek in manufacturing industries, the volume of new orders for consumer goods and materials industries, new businesses being formed, contracts and orders for new plants and equipment, new building permits for private housing units, changes in business inventories on hand and on order, changes in prices of key materials used in industrial processing, weekly unemployment insurance claims, and changes in business and consumer credit outstanding.

A major goal of the analysts who revised the composite index in 1975 was to remove any distortion that could creep in on account of inflation. This was a problem in 1973, when some of the key leading indicators continued to climb long after the economy, stripped of "growth" due merely to rising prices, had moved from an expansion phase to a period of contraction. The indicators that proved to be misleading, rather than leading, were mainly ones denominated in dollars—current dollars, as economists call them, the kind that you have in your wallet. Among these current-dollar indicators were corporate profits, contracts and orders for new plants and equipment, changes in business inventories, and new orders for durable goods. All were either removed from the composite index of leading indicators in the 1975 revision, or adjusted so as to be stated in terms of so-called constant dollars, which eliminates distortion due to price changes.

By the change, National Bureau economists hoped to avoid a repetition of the 1973 experience. At that time, the composite index—distorted by its current-dollar components—flashed no warning of the coming recession. It did not begin turning down until mid-1974, more than a half year after the start of the most severe business slump since before World War II. Government statisticians have reconstructed the revised composite index, first published in 1975, all the way back to 1948. Significantly, with its constant-dollar indicators, the new index started to warn of the approaching recession as early as July 1973, four months before the slump materialized.

It is clear that the use of constant-dollar indicators marks a major improvement in the composite index. A word of caution, however, should be given. In extreme economic situations— far more extreme than anything encountered in recent decades in the United States—constant-dollar statistics can behave strangely. It was noted in the second section of this chapter that the constant-dollar money supply—among the new indicators making up the revised composite index—actually rose for a time during the worst of the Great Depression. This was because prices were falling even faster than the money supply was shrinking. In an entirely different but equally extreme situation—Germany's runaway inflation in the early 1920s—the German money supply, adjusted for rising prices, contracted. The contraction occurred despite a flooding of the German economy with marks. Normally such a contraction of a country's "real" money supply would signal a business slump, with rising unemployment and extensive idle plant capacity. These things eventually did occur—but later, after the inflationary bubble was punctured by German authorities at the end of 1923. Earlier, unemployment dropped toward zero and factory operations were at a high level.

Any discussion of leading indicators would be incomplete without mentioning one other way in which it is possible to gain particularly early clues about the future course of the economy, especially before a downturn in business activity. We have observed that, besides leading indicators, economists have also assembled groups of "coincident" indicators, which move up or down coincidentally with overall business, as well as groups of "lagging" indicators, which tend to lag behind the broad economic trend. *Business Conditions Digest* contains composite indexes made up of selected indicators from these two categories, just as it contains a composite index of key leading indicators. The individual coincident and lagging indicators also appear in the monthly publication. Some are well known—such coincident indicators as the GNP and industrial production, and such lagging indicators as interest rates charged by banks and labor costs.

Taken individually, neither the coincident indicators nor the lagging indicators are particularly useful in providing early hints of future turns in the business cycle. However, Geoffrey Moore of the National Bureau has found that the two sets of indicators, used in tandem, combine to make a remarkably long-leading and reliable precursor of overall business. Specifically, Mr. Moore has constructed a ratio of the two composite indexes. It is a ratio of the coincident-composite index to the lagging-composite index.

The National Bureau economist has estimated that the ratio of the two composite indexes has begun to drop, on the average, about 13 months before recessions have set in. This lead is appreciably longer than the average warning given by the more widely known composite index of leading indicators. The ratio of the two indexes has been less useful—but still has been valuable—for signaling expansion periods. It has started to climb, on the average, about four months before economic recovery periods.

Mr. Moore is not at all surprised that the coincident-to-lagging ratio has so consistently presaged the movement of the economy as a whole. He explains that during a period of economic expansion, for instance, the ratio provides forecasters with a measure of how rapidly, in relation to general business activity, lagging indicators are climbing. These lagging indicators generally represent facets of the economic scene that by their nature tend to inhibit further growth as they rise—interest rates and labor costs are prime illustrations. Thus, their rapid increase would tend to depress Mr. Moore's ratio and signal economic constraints ahead for many businesses.

An example of the value of knowing which economic statistics provide useful indications of future business trends—and which do not—occurred in 1975. Someone trying to fathom the likely course of the slumping economy in, say, early June of that year could easily have become bewildered by economic headlines that at first glance seemed wildly contradictory. At the end of May, the government announced that its new index of leading indicators rose by a record amount in April, the latest month for which the index was available. But a few days later another government report showed that companies were scaling back their capital-spending plans sharply. And the next day it was announced that unemployment in May jumped to 9.2 percent of the labor force, the highest rate in 34 years.

Different economic yardsticks were giving off diametrically opposite signals. Accordingly, it was important to understand which yardsticks to monitor closely and which largely to disregard. Two that most decidedly are not indicative of the future economic course, especially in a time of deep recession, are capital-spending plans and the unemployment rate. Both tend to lag the general economic trend at such times. They often continue to worsen after business generally has started to improve.

Anyone attempting to stay abreast of the economic outlook in June, 1975, would have been wise to devote relatively little attention to those indicators and instead to keep an eye on the index of leading indicators. It rose a record 4.2 percent in April.

Its April level—95.3, on a base of 1967 = 100—was up from 91.5 in March and 90.6 in February. The February level marked the low point in a decline that began all the way back in July 1973, four months before the recession set in.

Anyone at all familiar with the record of the composite index would have found the rise since February most encouraging. Rarely had the index, after sinking to a recession low point, risen for two months and then started to decline again. The yardstick to have been watching was the leading-indicator index. The message that it flashed loud and clear in June 1975 was that the long recession was about over and that a period of renewed economic expansion seemed at hand. In fact, the economy embarked on an upturn that lasted until 1980, one of the longest expansions on record.

It is important to point out, however, that the magnitude of the record April rise in the composite index should not have been taken necessarily as evidence that a particularly strong, long-lasting economic upturn was ahead. The 4.2 percent rise in the composite index broke a record monthly increase of 3 percent set in June 1958—near the start of one of the shortest business expansions ever. There is broad agreement that, while leading indicators show the likely direction of the economy, they are not especially helpful in determining how sharp or enduring any change of course may turn out to be. That question can only be answered as a recovery progresses, by a careful scrutiny of major components of the economy.

"There's simply no telling how bad a recession is going to be until you're into it," says Geoffrey Moore. The vigor of an expansionary phase in the business cycle is, by the same token, difficult to predetermine.

The usefulness of the various economic indicators is also limited by the fact that they generally do not provide nearly as long a signal before recovery periods as before recessions. As noted, the composite index of leading indicators, on the average, has signaled recoveries by only four months, about half the length of the warning given prior to recessions. A few leading indicators, to be sure, have usually given much longer notice of recovery periods. Among these are the money supply, expressed as M-2 in constant dollars, and the series showing building permits for private housing units. Each indicator, on the average, has turned up eight months before a rise in overall business. Many leading indicators, in contrast, normally begin to climb only a month or two before the economy turns up. These include, among others, the average workweek, new orders for consumer goods, new business formations, and new orders for plants and machinery.

Despite these and other shortcomings, the various indicators do provide a remarkably convenient and uncomplicated means by which interested laymen, along with degree-laden economists, may intelligently keep abreast of—indeed, keep ahead of—the movement of the economy. You do not need to be an economist, and you do not need to know how to operate a computer.

As Geoffrey Moore has said, "Judgment will still have to be used in assessing the behavior of the indicators." Virtually all of these are available in *Business Conditions Digest,* a most valuable publication that may be obtained by writing for a yearly subscription to the Superintendent of Documents, U.S. Government Printing Office, Washington, D.C. 20402.

As we will see in the next chapter, there are far more expensive ways to try to keep abreast of the economic outlook. None, we submit, is better than simply doing it yourself, with the help of a daily newspaper, such as *The Wall Street Journal* or, if you live in the New York area, *The New York Times*—plus the monthly issues of BCD. The effort requires remarkably little of your time. You may also avoid, in the process, a lot of very bad forecasts.

To rely on economic indicators, in the final analysis, is to rely on common sense. Geoffrey Moore, writing in the January 1975 issue of *Scientific American,* discussed, among other things, the reason that such statistical series as housing starts, new orders for machinery, and contracts for new construction projects all usually show an increase several months before the economy in general picks up. "It takes time to build a house or a factory or a turbine," he observed. "The actual production or completion or shipping usually lags behind the orders and contracts." It is that "actual production," of course, that determines the overall level of business activity in the country—in effect, the particular phase of the cycle that business happens to be in. As we have seen, we can be reasonably sure that business will be always in one phase or the other, expanding or contracting.

CHAPTER 8

TRUE AND FALSE PROPHETS

It is possible, we have observed, to gain valuable insights into the likely future behavior of the economy by simply keeping track of various economic indicators. Moreover, one need not be a degree-laden economist to follow these indicators and, using them, to ascertain the probable direction of the business cycle.

We have seen, in effect, that you can do it yourself. The necessary statistical information is readily available. And it can be assessed and used to form sound conclusions—without the need of expertise.

The layman who seeks perspective on the economy and its likely course should also make an effort, however, to peruse at least a few of the economic forecasts that regularly emanate from experts. For there assuredly is no shortage of highly trained economists who make a business—frequently high priced and highly profitable—of monitoring every statistical series mentioned in this book, and many more besides. They apply their expertise to digest all the data and then come up with periodic forecasts of how the economic trend is likely to develop. The forecasts may range over developments in coming months or years or even decades. Mostly, however, forecasters limit their predictions to periods not beyond 12 months.

Within that span, they generally provide detailed estimates regarding such matters as the likely level of the GNP and the real GNP, the likely rate of unemployment, probable changes in the consumer-price index, and so on. One area that economists often eschew in their forecasts is the stock market. As we have noted, share-price indexes can behave in the short run in a highly volatile fashion, and most economists are understandably wary about trying to predict such volatile movements in any precise detail.

LOTS OF PROPHETS

The layman who wishes to keep abreast of expert views on the economic future should have no difficulty. The daily newspapers contain forecasts. Major banks and securities firms employ analysts who produce frequent appraisals of the business outlook. Often, these forecasts are freely available to customers who merely express an interest in obtaining them. Corporations also employ forecasters whose main job is to advise top executives about general business prospects. Often this advice is kept within the corporation. But some major concerns do publish their forecasts. Prudential Life and Merrill Lynch are examples. A notable exception is IBM, the computer giant, whose economists are among the more reticent forecasters in the nation.

Among major banks, Chase Manhattan, Morgan Guaranty, Manufacturers Hanovers, and Citibank, all in New York, First Chicago, and Bank of America turn out a variety of material on a reasonably regular basis that appraises the economic climate. Morgan Guaranty, particularly, prides itself on the excellence of its economics department and the profusion of material, much of it readily available to the public, that the department turns out each month.

Most prominent business forecasters make at least some of their reports freely available to major newspapers, if not to the public in general. But only a fraction of this material actually finds its way into the financial pages. Many newspapers devote only limited space to any sort of economic news. Their business coverage often consists largely of reporting the latest stock and bond prices. Some forecasts do find their way, fortunately, into such newspapers as *The Wall Street Journal, The New York Times, The Washington Post,* and *The Los Angeles Times.* But even in these newspapers, what appears is usually a minuscule fraction of what is received in newsrooms around the country. If its editors so chose, *The Wall Street Journal,* my employer, could print nothing but economic predictions on all of its pages every day of the week. Wisely, its editors have long exercised considerable discretion in deciding which forecasts should be run in whole or in part each day and which should best be relegated to the wastebasket.

One type of forecast is rarely relegated to *The Wall Street Journal*'s wastebasket. That is the forecast made by a high government official, such as the President, the Chairman of his Council of Economic Advisers, the Treasury Secretary, or the Chairman of the Federal Reserve Board. The reasoning among most editors—quite logically—is that such individuals are in positions where they can actually influence future economic activity, and this ability lends considerable weight to their forecasts. If the Chairman of the Federal Reserve Board says that he believes the economy is about to move from a recessionary phase to a period of expansion, the prediction is deemed highly significant, because the Fed Chairman actually has the power to spur economic growth through adopting a more expansionary monetary policy. He also may be privy to information about the economy not yet generally available.

Suffice it to say that the interested layman who wishes to expand his perspective on the business outlook—gained, one would hope, through a careful observation of the appropriate economic indicators—may do so by keeping a tab on the various forecasts reported in the major newspapers. He may further broaden his perspective by obtaining, often at no charge, forecasts made by selected banks, securities concerns, and large corporations.

Different forecasters use different forecasting methods. Some go through a more elaborate version of the process that anyone familiar with the important indicators described in this book can readily perform. Others go far beyond scrutinizing the indicators and set up esoteric mathematical equations—"models" of the overall economy, in effect, constructed with such building blocks as the GNP and the inflation rate.

These equations are fed into computers which, in short order, spew out all sorts of information about the future shape of the economy. These "econometric" forecasts (which reflect the merging of mathematics, statistics, and economics) can be especially useful to individual corporations; computers can be set to predict economic developments down to such details as the number of shoes likely to be sold during a six-month period. Such information, while of dubious interest or use to most citizens, would presumably be of considerable concern to a shoe manufacturer.

The differing methods that forecasters use to reach their estimates of the business outlook are noted by the National Bureau's Mr. Moore, who—perhaps wisely—does exceedingly little forecasting himself. "Analysis of economic indicators is one way of assessing" the economic outlook, he says, and "econometric models of the business-cycle process are another."

I should emphasize that there is no substitute for keeping abreast of the important statistics yourself, and trying to understand how the business cycle may develop. For it is a fact that many of the business prophets are occasionally more than slightly inaccurate in their forecasts. Moreover, like the rest of us, forecasters for various reasons do not always proclaim in public what they may be telling their employers in private. This is all the more reason that you should, basically, try to do it yourself, as far as assessing the economic outlook is concerned.

SHORTCOMINGS

Various studies have been conducted in recent years to try to determine precisely how accurate business forecasters have been. The studies show a considerably less than perfect record. Beware of the forecaster who does not employ an ample amount of modesty and caution in predicting the economic course. The proper approach should be along the line used by Gilbert Heebner of Philadelphia National Bank. Making a "midyear outlook" report in June 1975, the economist began: "Economists should approach the current midyear forecast with an extra measure of humility. For it was only a year ago that the profession erred so badly in failing to predict the sharp drop that began last fall." Mr. Heebner maintained that "it is always a healthy exercise for an economist to ask: If his or her forecast should err—a not-infrequent occurrence—in which direction is it likely to err, and why?"

A survey conducted by *Business Week* in December 1973 makes clear how badly highly trained forecasters can occasionally err. The magazine published the estimates of 32 prominent forecasters for the economy in 1974. Among other details, the survey showed each one's forecast for the real GNP and for price changes during 1974. Only one of the 32—and he deserves to be named: A. Gary Shilling, then at White, Weld—forecast a decline in the real GNP during 1974. Mr. Shilling predicted a 1.5 percent drop in that coincident indicator: in fact, it fell nearly twice that much during the year.

Many of the 31 other forecasts predicted substantial increases in the real GNP.

Even more lamentable was the group's record on the price front. In 1974. prices actually rose more than 10 percent, on the average. But none of the 32 forecasters anticipated double-digit inflation. The highest rate of price increase forecast by anyone was 7.5 percent. One unfortunate fellow, a professor of economics at Princeton University who relied heavily on econometric techniques, forecast a price climb of only 4.7 percent in 1974. The same forecaster also predicted that the real GNP would rise a healthy 3.5 percent in the year.

To be fair, 1974 was a particularly difficult year for forecasters to envisage. As noted in the previous chapter, inflation badly distorted the movement of leading indicators denominated in dollars.

Over longer intervals, various studies show that the track records of most forecasters are reasonably respectable. In late 1974, the Boston Federal Reserve Bank studied the records of seven prominent forecasting organizations over a four-year period. The Boston Fed found that "despite unusually large forecasting errors recently, the best forecasters have been able to anticipate the growth of GNP and real GNP with an average absolute error of 1 percent."

In the January 1975 issue of a business review published by Morgan Guaranty Trust, Geoffrey Moore reviewed the forecasting records of government economists as well as those of many analysts employed by private businesses. He concluded that "the two groups seem to use the same crystal ball." It is clear, he stated, that "economists can point to a creditable performance over the years in forecasting output." However, he added, "in forecasting prices, clearly there is much room for improvement."

The National Bureau analyst also noted that the forecasters in both the groups have tended over the years "to err in their predictions on the side of optimism—both tend to overestimate output and to underestimate the probable increase in the price level." Certainly, undue optimism prevailed in that *Business Week* survey in December 1973.

This tendency toward overoptimism is important to bear in mind when one peruses forecasts. One need not look far to understand why the tendency exists. An anecdote involving a major securities concern suggests one explanation. It involves the aforementioned Gary Shilling.

I first came to know Mr. Shilling back in the late 1960s, when he was chief economist—at the astoundingly young age of 29—for the nation's largest and, in the view of many, most prestigious Wall Street securities firm, Merrill Lynch, Pierce, Fenner and Smith. John Allan, then a reporter on *The New York Times* and a former colleague at *The Wall Street Journal*, had mentioned Mr. Shilling to me as a man who correctly predicted, almost to the day, a generally unexpected devaluation of the British pound. This was no mean achievement back in the years when key currency-exchange rates were fixed in relation to one another, and therefore unlikely to change from one week to the next, as often happens now.

Appropriately impressed, I made it a point to get in touch with this bright young analyst. By 1969 I had become a staunch admirer of his forecasting abilities. Little did I imagine that this admiration would eventually place Mr. Shilling in a most uncomfortable situation at Merrill Lynch.

The trouble began on a bright December morning, a day or two before Christmas, 1969. The Merrill Lynch economist called to wish me a merry Christmas and also to express his not-so-merry doubts about the country's economic prospects. He told me, among other things, that he fully anticipated—and I use his adjective—a "major" recession just ahead. This was a considerably more gloomy position than that held by most economic forecasters at the time. The consensus was that no recession impended. Even relatively pessimistic members of the forecasting fraternity felt any slowdown that might occur surely would constitute only a mild interruption in the ongoing business expansion. At least that is what was generally stated publicly.

Mr. Shilling, of course, turned out to be eminently correct. A major recession, as we noted earlier, did indeed begin in late 1969, and it persisted and deepened for about a year. The Merrill Lynch economist's prescient warning appeared under my byline on December 26, 1969. The headline read: "Merrill Lynch Chief Economist Sees Business Headed into Major Recession."

Donald T. Regan, who ran Merrill Lynch at that time, long before he joined the Reagan administration in Washington, was highly upset to find his chief economist predicting publicly a major recession—and, no shrinking violet, he let Mr. Shilling know about it in blunt terms. The economist recalls, among other things, that his bonus—in those days, an important part of yearly compensation at many Wall Street firms—was reduced sharply a short time after the recession forecast was published. In the ensuing weeks, as the recession materialized, I noticed that Mr. Shilling's forecasts became rarer and rarer and, when they did sporadically surface, seemed blander and more cautious. He found himself involved in a variety of in-house projects, including special assignments for Mr. Regan that allowed him little time for economic forecasting. Eventually, he found himself no longer the firm's chief economist but merely one of several economists assigned not to the parent company but to a recently acquired investment-advisory subsidiary, Lionel D. Edie & Company. Soon thereafter, Mr. Shilling quit his Merrill Lynch employment. He became chief economist at White, Weld, a Wall Street securities firm eventually acquired by Merrill Lynch, at which point Mr. Shilling left to start his own firm. (In fairness, it should be noted that a Merrill Lynch spokesman says it was not the substance of the Shilling forecast but the manner in which it was released—prematurely to the press—that "irked everyone." As for the reduced bonus, the spokesman says Merrill Lynch suffered a sharp decline in its earnings that year.)

Still, the lesson for anyone who follows the forecasts of economists employed by private businesses seems plain enough. Be aware that such economists can easily antagonize their bosses if they sound too pessimistic about the business outlook—at least in public. Ridiculous as it may seem, many business people apparently believe that gloomy forecasts can actually create a gloomy economy. By the same token, there are many executives who seem to think that by producing optimistic forecasts, economists can somehow raise the general level of business activity.

If there is any truth at all in such ideas, the amount must be minuscule. In any event, it is a wise procedure to bear in mind the pressures that may force some economists, who may actually be pessimistic about business prospects, to remain silent—or, much worse, to sound more optimistic in public than they feel in private.

The same tendency toward overoptimism, not surprisingly, prevails among forecasters employed by the administration that happens to be in power in Washington. With notable—and noble—exceptions, such officials invariably try to be more sanguine than economic facts may justify. Typical of this habit were the repeated predictions of Herbert Stein, President Nixon's chief economic adviser in the early 1970s, that inflation would soon begin to abate. Again and again, the Nixon economist told the electorate what it presumably enjoyed hearing—that inflation would soon ease. And again and again he turned out to be wrong. Rather than abating, inflation intensified painfully during Mr. Stein's tenure in Washington.

After departing Washington, the economist took up duties as an occasional columnist for *The Wall Street Journal*. Writing as a private citizen, he seemed far more concerned about the possibility of worsening inflation than he appeared to be during his speech-making days at the White House, when warnings of a worsening price spiral were fully warranted but not forthcoming.

There are, in addition, occasional instances where a forecast may be unduly pessimistic because of political pressures on the forecaster. I recall such a situation in early 1971, when the economy was just beginning to pull out of the 1969 to 1970 recession. A prominent economics professor, who had served as an adviser to President Johnson and was still closely tied to the Democratic party, was publicly lambasting the Nixon administration for what the professor claimed were woefully inadequate policies that would surely perpetuate the recession. If taken seriously, these forecasts would have chilled any optimism about business prospects that a layman might have acquired, say, by simply following the climb of various leading indicators at that time.

Quite by chance, I discovered that the professor also served as a consultant to a New York-based brokerage house, one of whose executives is an old friend. My stockbroker friend, I was aware, was reasonably—and, as things turned out, rightly—optimistic about the economic outlook. I asked him how this optimism squared with the obvious gloom expressed by the firm's consultant. My friend's reply: "We know that in his public statements he has been sharply critical of Nixon's economic performance, charging that the President isn't doing nearly enough to get the economy out of the recession. However, his private advice to us, for which we pay him a considerable retainer, has sounded like this—the Nixon team has done a good job of getting inflation under control without letting the recession get too deep, the business outlook is very good, with a prolonged period of economic expansion in prospect, and you should therefore get your clients invested in sound stocks."

A similar episode of more recent vintage involves Senator Hubert Humphrey, in his highly visible role as chairman of the Joint Economic Committee of Congress. In mid-1975, when the leading indicators unmistakably pointed upward toward a recovery period, Senator Humphrey, in his committee role, issued a particularly gloomy appraisal of the outlook. The appraisal came on the heels of a Labor Department report that the nation's jobless rate had jumped to 9.2 percent. He deplored the unemployment rise as a harbinger of still worse economic times ahead. Among other things, he gloomily forecast that "there is no employment rise in sight."

In fact, a recovery in employment was already under way.

The same report that showed a rise in the unemployment rate to 9.2 percent also disclosed, in the fine print, a 316,000 jump in employment, on top of a 237,000 employment increase the month before. The Humphrey statement made no mention of this rise in employment. As we saw earlier, employment changes can tell more about general economic conditions than changes in the jobless rate.

The message is clear. Anyone attempting to keep abreast of the economic outlook through observing published forecasts should do so gingerly. If the forecaster, like Senator Humphrey, happens to be a political opponent of the administration in the White House, be wary of excessive pessimism. If the forecaster, like Herbert Stein, is employed by the White House, look out for too much optimism. And if the forecaster works for a profit-making organization whose boss may believe—rightly or wrongly—that gloomy forecasts can hurt business, again be wary of over-optimism.

CREDENTIALS

Before leaving the matter of forecasting, a few words are in order about credentials. All through this chapter, I have stressed that most widely followed forecasters are "degree-laden" and "highly trained." A primary message of this book, of course, is to emphasize precisely that you do not need to be "degree-laden" or "highly trained" to appraise the economic scene intelligently. It is true that most successful forecasters are indeed laden with degrees in economics. But one should bear in mind that there are major exceptions. This can be readily illustrated by recalling predictions made in 1973 by two widely followed but remarkably disparate forecasters.

The forecasting game, like many other endeavors, attracts wildly diverse players. The disparate forecasters that I have in mind are Robert H. Parks, serving in 1973 as chief economist of Blyth Eastman Dillon & Company, a large, well-known New York securities concern, and Harry D. Schultz, the publisher of an economic newsletter with several thousand loyal subscribers. The credentials of the two forecasters are strikingly dissimilar.

Bob Parks' credentials are, to say the least, impressive. The "doctor" that he uses before his name is well earned. His credentials include a doctorate and a master's degree from the University of Pennsylvania, a bachelor's degree from Swarthmore, and professorships at two universities.

Not so with Harry Schultz. He once told a *Wall Street Journal* reporter—who accepted it—that the "doctor" he uses before his name reflects a doctorate he received from St. Lawrence University in New York State. But his name is utterly unknown to officials at St. Lawrence. "We find no indication that one Mr. Harry Schultz ever attended St. Lawrence University at any time or that he ever received an honorary degree from this university," declares an official of the Canton, New York, institution. It does appear that Harry Schultz did spend a couple of years at City College of Los Angeles, where he majored not in economics or finance, but journalism.

So, the question arises: Which man's view of the economic future would you tend to heed—that of Dr. Parks or that of "Dr." Schultz?

In mid-1973, if you had been listening to Bob Parks over the past year or so, you would probably have kept much of your money invested in the U.S. stock market—and taken your lumps along with most investors. As we saw earlier in the *Business Week* survey, Bob Parks assuredly was not alone among respected analysts in 1973 in his optimism about general business prospects.

"Dr." Schultz, on the other hand, was dispensing some uncannily prescient advice to his subscribers in 1973. His letters dripped in gloom about the economic outlook. One suggested "portfolio" of his, consisting wholly of South African gold-mining shares, had appreciated more than 200 percent since the beginning of 1972. Another, made up largely of securities from such countries as France and Switzerland, but without a single share of U.S. stock, had climbed about 20 percent just since the start of 1973, a period in which prices of most U.S. stocks dropped sharply.

Looking ahead in mid-1973, with much rough economic weather to come, Bob Parks remained relatively optimistic. One Parks appraisal of economic prospects, for example, expressed the belief that "this expansion [of economic activity] will turn out to be one of the longest in U.S. history." He was utterly wrong, of course; the expansion ended in November of that very year. He also opined that President Nixon's actions on the price front [to initiate a series of price-control moves in August 1971] "visibly and believably" strengthened the country's "attack on inflation." In fact, inflation worsened severely in the year or so after the Parks forecast.

"Dr." Harry Schultz, in mid-1973, saw the outlook differently. One report, almost comical in the degree of its pessimism, began: "Civilization, as we know it, is crumbling." Regarding the U.S. stock market, he advised "short positions." He commented that "even in 1930 there were rallies." Regarding his favorite metal, gold—a traditional haven for economic pessimists—he appeared confident that its price would be heading upward in the months to come—and it most certainly did rise.

The gloom expressed by Harry Schultz in 1973 may have been more than a little excessive; publishers of economic newsletters often tend to be overly pessimistic, apparently in the belief that this tactic attracts more subscribers. In any case, that Harry Schultz was largely correct about the economic future in 1973 provides a valuable lesson for anyone who may be tempted to pick forecasters solely on the basis of how many economic degrees they possess or how well known their firms may be.

Altogether, it is clear that to follow economic forecasts blindly is a risky undertaking. Forecasters with impressive credentials can be entirely wrong about the outlook, while forecasters with seemingly unimpressive credentials—or credentials that turn out to be false—can prove to be correct.

A few successful economists are so wary about trying to predict the precise movement of the business cycle that they simply refuse to issue detailed forecasts at all.

One such analyst was Edward C. Harwood, founder of an economic research concern in Great Barrington, Massachusetts. In elaborating on his position, the economist once explained that

we do not join in the annual forecasting derby that is so popular among economists, pseudo-economists, and business analysts near the beginning of each new year. . . . Neither we nor anyone else that we know of has developed a scientific basis for predicting with a useful degree of accuracy the levels that gross national product, the industrial production index, stock market averages or other measures of economic activity will reach six months or a year in the future. Of course, computers will provide such projections with remarkable speed, but the final printout of a computer is no more accurate in foreseeing the future than are the assumptions and guesses of the individuals who develop the input program. Also, because we have not discovered any reliable method for predicting these short-term fluctuations in the various aspects of economic activity, we do not attempt to give trading advice to investors or recommend frequent changes in an investment portfolio in the hope of making quick profits.

Mr. Harwood contented himself by assuming that inflation, despite occasional periods of abatement, would continue to worsen and erode the dollar's buying power. He believed that the prudent investor should concentrate on ways to limit this erosion, rather than worry about whether the business cycle happens to be in an up-phase or a down-phase.

Such a strategy, if nothing else, protected Mr. Harwood from the embarrassment, suffered in 1973 by Bob Parks, of producing woefully wrong forecasts. It also kept him comfortably aloof from the nasty sort of backbiting that unhappily pervades the forecasting game. I once obtained a front-row view of this widespread practice among forecasters. I had mentioned in a *Wall Street Journal* column in mid-1974 that Gary Shilling anticipated an unemployment rate of 8 percent or more in coming months. At the time, with actual unemployment just above 5 percent of the labor force, it was a rather daring forecast for anyone to make, even an economist with Mr. Shilling's good track record.

Soon after the column appeared, I received an angry letter from Mike Evans of Chase Econometrics. Mr. Evans, whom I barely knew, attacked at length Mr. Shilling's competence as a forecaster. Among other charges, the Chase Econometrics president declared that "I view his 8 percent unemployment rate forecast as being [much too high] and dead wrong." Less than six months after the Evans letter arrived, the unemployment rate crossed above 8 percent, and less than a year after the letter, the rate stood at 9.2 percent.

Perhaps the one thing more embarrassing for a forecaster than issuing a dead-wrong forecast is to be dead wrong in claiming that a colleague's forecast is dead wrong. That is the sort of embarrassment that Mr. Harwood in his Great Barrington office, in the rolling hills of western Massachusetts, was in no danger of suffering.

CHAPTER 9

THE GLOBAL CONNECTION

John Donne, the seventeenth-century British poet, once observed that "no man is an island, entire of it self." He went on to caution that one should "never send to know for whom the bell tolls; it tolls for thee."

Thus far, our attention has been focused largely on ways of gauging the approximate level and likely future development of economic activity within the United States. Had this book been written, say, in 1950, there would have been little need for this chapter. The U.S. economy, in those bygone days, could have been appraised well enough through simply remaining abreast of appropriate economic gauges designed to measure the health of U.S. business.

The U.S. economy in those years, in an economic sense, was still a sort of island. It was an island in that its size and strength, in relation to other economies, was so overwhelming that it was largely impervious to economic developments elsewhere. It was an island in another sense—on account of the exceptional monetary arrangements under which international business was transacted. These arrangements, as we will see, were highly advantageous to the United States. For many years, they served to insulate the country from some of the nastier consequences of its own economic policies.

Now, a very different economic world has emerged, in which no important country can be an economic island. When the bell tolls now, it does so for all the major economies. Nowadays, any attempt to understand the U.S. economy necessitates keeping track of economic developments abroad as well as at home. This can be easily done—though it must be said that few other countries maintain the profusion of reasonably reliable economic yardsticks that U.S. analysts have managed to assemble.

In this chapter, we will try to trace the increasing interdependence of the U.S. economy and those elsewhere. We will, further, offer some suggestions on how best to follow the diverse, often puzzling foreign picture.

NO ISLAND

In the fourth chapter, we briefly discussed the international value of the U.S. dollar as a useful barometer of the health of the American economy. It was noted, among other things, that the dollar's international value—that is, its price in terms of other currencies—nowadays moves up or down largely in response to everchanging forces of supply and demand. The dollar tends to appreciate in terms of other currencies when demand for it is on the rise. And it tends to decline in terms of other currencies when foreign demand for it sags. In effect, the dollar's international value tends to "float"—to use an expression of economists—in relation to other currencies.

This floating arrangement has existed only since 1971. In earlier years after World War II, the international value of the U.S. dollar did not float. Instead, it was arbitrarily fixed, under international agreement, at a level of $35 per ounce of gold. This so-called fixed-rate system was set up at an international monetary conference held at Bretton Woods, New Hampshire, in 1944. Under the system, U.S. officials were to try to keep the value of the dollar fixed at $35 per ounce of gold, and other major countries were to try to keep the value of their particular currencies fixed in terms of the dollar.

The upshot, at least in theory, was that all currencies were fixed in terms of one another. The United States with a huge supply of gold at the end of World War II, stood ready to buy or sell the yellow metal in transactions with other governments at a rate of $35 per ounce. At the same time, other governments stood ready to buy or sell dollars in such a way as to maintain the agreed-upon fixed relationships between their currencies and the dollar. A commercial bank in Country X would, under the fixed-rate system, turn in dollars to Country X's central bank and, in return, receive googols, the Country X currency, at whatever happened to be the fixed rate of exchange between the dollar and the googol.

As things developed, this fixed-rate arrangement served to insulate the United States from inflationary pressures that might otherwise have developed within the American economy. Instead, these pressures were transmitted out of the United States and developed abroad. Exactly how this transmission occurred can best be illustrated, perhaps, by recalling events in West Germany in 1971, the year in which the Bretton Woods system of fixed rates fell apart.

On May 5 of that year, the Bundesbank, West Germany's central bank, stopped buying dollars for marks and, in effect, let the dollar float downward in relation to the mark. By so doing, the German government abandoned Bretton Woods procedure. In the 48 hours beforehand, West German officials later explained, the Bundesbank had been obliged by Bretton Woods rules to buy more than $2 billion at the fixed dollar–mark rate of exchange, issuing marks for the U.S. currency. They complained bitterly at the time that such forced buying of dollars for marks was exacerbating inflation in their country by causing the German money supply to rise at about twice the desired rate.

The West German experience of May 1971, illustrates how inflation could be exported under the Bretton Woods arrangement. Dollars poured into Germany far in excess of what German officials deemed healthy for their country's economy. Otmar Emminger, a governor of the Bundesbank, estimated at the time that West Germany's money supply was growing at an annual rate of more than 20 percent in the spring of 1971, a period when a monetary growth rate of about 10 percent appeared appropriate.

Under Bretton Woods procedure, West German officials could have asked the U.S. government for gold, at the $35 price, for the unwanted dollars at the Bundesbank—piling up there as Americans continued to spend and invest heavily in West Germany. In practice, however, West Germany—as well as other foreign countries similarly inundated—was hesitant to make such a request because, bluntly, it had become increasingly clear that

America's dwindling gold supply could no longer meet the potential demands of dollar-holders abroad.

The inevitable result of this bind was the West German decision, followed by similar ones elsewhere, to stop buying dollars for marks. Later in 1971, in another inevitable move, the United States officially abandoned its long-standing pledge to buy or sell gold at the $35 figure.

Now, since the Bretton Woods system has collapsed, currency values float daily in relation to one another, largely in response to the forces of supply and demand. No government is obliged to swallow American dollars at a fixed rate of exchange if dollars pile up there. Now, when the Federal Reserve's monetary policy becomes overly expansionary, much of the resulting inflationary pressure must stay home. Such inflation no longer may be readily exported, as before, to such places as West Germany. Accordingly, excessive dollars now will more quickly generate domestic inflation. Under today's circumstances. the dollar's value in international currency markets would be likelier to drop if Fed policy is overly expansionary. And any such drop would likely intensify inflationary pressures at home, inasmuch as it would make imported goods costlier for Americans and spur demand for U.S.-made products abroad.

The precise inflationary impact of any sharp rise in the U.S. money supply, to be sure, would depend on a variety of imponderables. These range from how cleanly the dollar is allowed to float in relation to other currencies—without interference in international-currency markets by central-banking authorities—to how expansionary the policies of other governments happen to be. The international value of the dollar, to illustrate, would presumably hold up better if policies of rapid monetary growth happen to be pursued in other countries. As a result of the change from fixed to floating rates, those who determine U.S. economic policy nowadays must proceed more cautiously than in the Bretton Woods era. They must keep a sharper watch on economic developments abroad—and the same applies for the individual who wishes to keep abreast.

A few words should perhaps be inserted here to point out that considerable disagreement exists among economists over whether a fixed-rate system or a floating-rate arrangement is more inflationary for the world as a whole. Proponents of a fixed-rate system point to the fact that inflation in most countries worsened considerably after the Bretton Woods system collapsed in 1971.

Analysts who favor floating rates contend that much of the world's post-1971 inflation derives from practices in effect during the Bretton Woods years, when the United States was pumping all those dollars abroad. In fact, these analysts blame much of the post-1971 inflation precisely on the huge hoard of American dollars that accumulated abroad under the fixed-rate system. Many of these dollars, it is observed, still are on deposit in European banks and elsewhere, under the label of Eurodollars. It is generally agreed that these Eurodollars—probably exceeding the $1 trillion mark, but no one knows by how much—contributed greatly to inflationary pressure throughout the world in earlier postwar years. Advocates of floating exchange rates argue that the pileup of Eurodollars never would have reached such proportions without the fixed-rate system.

Whatever the merits of the opposing viewpoints, the fact is that in today's world of floating rates, the U.S. government cannot pursue inflationary policies with impunity. As economist Milton Friedman once observed, "Fixed rates allow inflationary policies to be disguised."

The advent of floating exchange rates is merely one manifestation of the rising economic interdependence of the major economies. This interdependence shows up in other ways as well. U.S. foreign trade figures provide one illustration. In 1960, U.S. exports amounted to only about 5 percent of the country's gross national product, and U.S. imports constituted an even smaller percentage of the GNP. By 1974, as international commerce continued to expand extra rapidly, U.S. exports alone amounted to about 10 percent of the GNP, twice the 1960 rate. More recently, this has risen to about 12 percent, with an even higher import rate. Clearly, foreign trade has become an important factor in the country's economic picture. Accordingly, a sharp drop in the country's export volume today would unquestionably have a much more severe impact on American jobs and general prosperity than such a drop would have had, say, in 1960. In the same manner, as U.S. imports have risen, so has the importance of the American economy to many businesses and workers abroad.

In a recent period, roughly 25 percent of cars sold in the United States were manufactured abroad. This remarkably high rate leaves little doubt that any severe cutback in U.S. spending for automobiles could have serious economic consequences in auto-producing countries abroad.

Most forecasters expect the role of foreign trade within the U.S. economic picture to continue to expand. Otto Eckstein of Data Resources once remarked that "the health of the world economy will be of increasing importance to the United States" in the years ahead.

Other statistics underline the rising economic importance of international investment flows, as well as international trade, to the United States. In some recent years, over 20 percent of private investments made in the United States were by foreigners. That compares with a figure of only 7 percent in 1963 and less than 4 percent in 1958. A similar rise in foreign investing in various government-type securities, such as Treasury bills, is also apparent from other statistics.

The considerable role that foreign investors now occupy on the U.S. economic stage means, among other things, that business decisions affecting American jobs and prosperity more often are being made by foreigners. It is far likelier today that a decision, say, to build a new American automobile plant may depend, at least in part, on economic and political conditions in West Germany or Japan or France or Sweden, or even Taiwan or South Korea.

A major illustration of this interdependence spreading beyond just the highly industrialized economies occurred in 1973. That was when the Middle Eastern oil-producing countries demanded—with resounding success—sharply higher prices for their oil. The move made clear the extent to which key economies, including the exceedingly powerful U.S. economy, had become linked to business and political decisions made far from New York or London or Frankfurt or Paris or Tokyo.

The decision to increase petroleum prices so sharply—and

even for a while to withhold petroleum shipments—caused un-
imagined economic repercussions in the United States and elsewhere. There were, of course, the long lines at gasoline stations.
Families in New York saw their electricity bills soar. Executives
in Detroit saw sales of their high-powered, gas-guzzling cars
plunge. As noted earlier, it can be argued convincingly that the
deep recession which started in November 1973 set in much
sooner than might otherwise have been the case. Many economists believe that, without the oil squeeze, the 1970 to 1973 economic expansion would have kept going until at least mid-1974.

Impressed by the success of the oil-producing countries in
raising petroleum prices, countries producing a wide range of
other important industrial raw materials—for instance bauxite,
used in making aluminum—began driving harder and harder
bargains in their trade negotiations with such commodity-con-
suming industrial powers as the United States. These other
raw-materials producers did not enjoy the same high degree of
success as the oil producers. Few materials are as vital to the
industrial countries as oil. However, to the extent that they were
successful at all, this surely affected economic developments in
the United States and other highly developed nations.

The other side of the coin is that the materials-producing
lands themselves became more important customers for manufactured goods and technological expertise supplied by such
countries as the United States. This is because their wealth rose
along with the rising revenues that their raw materials brought
from the United States and elsewhere. The inflow of money
tended to spur spending in these areas, which remained relatively undeveloped in economic terms. Not surprisingly, U.S. exports to the oil-rich countries of the Middle East rose sharply.

A high degree of economic intertwining is already evident
in the fact that the business cycles of the major economies appear to be closely in phase with one another. This has not always
been the case.

In the years fairly soon after World War II, in contrast to
nowadays, the economies of most countries moved in the same
direction at the same time relatively rarely. America's industrial

output index slumped in 1960, for example, and yet industrial output in many major West European countries climbed briskly during that period. More recently, economic activity declined in France in 1968, in Italy in 1969, and in the United Kingdom in 1972—without concurrent economic declines in such other key areas as the United States or Japan.

Such disparity, however, has been diminishing in recent years. Indeed, the 1973 to 1975 recession appears to have set in at approximately the same time in most industrial lands. Not all the countries entered recessions precisely in November 1973, the month designated by the National Bureau as the start of the slump in the United States. But various statistics do indicate that business activity outside the United States generally began to contract within a few months, on one side or the other, of the November date. Among countries whose economies slumped around this time were Canada, France, West Germany, Italy, and Japan. Together, they account for a considerable portion of worldwide business activity.

This remarkably uniform behavior, in the view of many analysts, reflects mainly the aforementioned growth of international trade and investment, and the consequent intertwining of different economies. Exports, for instance, play an even larger economic role in most countries nowadays than in the United States. A prime example is West Germany, where export sales rose in a recent 10-year period from 21 percent of the West German gross national product to 30 percent.

Looking ahead, the consensus view is that in the long run the interdependence of the major economies will continue and grow, and that this interdependence will gradually extend as well to most less-developed economies. Increasing uniformity of world-wide economic developments if forecast by most economists, though in the shorter term they worry over protectionist pressures in the United States Congress as well as in governments abroad.

Such projections emphasize the importance of trying to keep abreast of economic trends beyond the boundaries of the United States. To noneconomists, that may seem a forbidding endeavor. However, it is not nearly as difficult as one may imagine. Much of the useful information is readily available. In addition, governments and private analysts in many countries are striving to improve the quality and expand the quantity of economic data.

WATCHING THE WORLD

We have observed the growing economic interdependence of the major industrial countries. We have seen that good times in the United States or West Germany or Japan are likelier nowadays to coincide with good times elsewhere. And, unfortunately, the same thing can be said about bad times. It is not surprising, in view of this interdependence, that a major effort is under way to assemble data that bears on the economic outlook in foreign areas, as well as in the United States.

Students of the U.S. economy, we have seen, have long had available statistics that indicate in abundant detail the health and likely course of American business. One collection of such data is, as noted earlier, *Business Conditions Digest,* the Commerce Department's monthly publication.

The publication also contains important international statistics—industrial production, consumer-price reports, and stock-market movements for more than a half dozen major countries abroad. These statistics provide a simple, fast way for the interested layman to keep up to date on key foreign trends. However, absent from *Business Conditions Digest* is a variety of data that might clearly suggest, for example, whether economic activity in West Germany is likely to accelerate or slow.

One effort to fill this void has been undertaken by the Center for International Business Cycle Research at Columbia University. Economists there, directed by Geoffrey Moore, do on an international scale what *Business Conditions Digest* has done so well for so long on the American scene. They publish a monthly report containing leading-indicator indexes for nine major industrial nations abroad.

The effort to set up a regular publication of international economic data is by no means unique. Other efforts are under way. The St. Louis Federal Reserve Bank, for example, brings out a quarterly publication that provides statistical information on major foreign countries, as well as the United States. Covered are trends in international trade, production, employment, prices and, most importantly, the money supply. The quarterly publication may be obtained by writing to the St. Louis Fed's research department at Post Office Box 442, St. Louis, Missouri 63166.

Another noteworthy project is the attempt by economists at the University of Pennsylvania's Wharton School to construct a computer-based model of international economic activity. The econometric model, appropriately enough, has been christened Project Link.

Still another source of important foreign statistics is a monthly publication of the International Monetary Fund. Called *International Financial Statistics,* it offers a vast range of data covering the organization's more than 100 member nations. The particular advantage of this publication over, say, the Commerce Department's *Business Conditions Digest* is that it also contains economic information, in varying detail, about so-called less-developed countries. It shows, for instance, that Mauritania's trade balance was in the red to the tune of about one billion *ouguiyas*—the Mauritanian currency—during the third quarter of 1972. Such economic details are hardly of widespread interest to most Americans. But they do illustrate the scope of the IMF publication. It may be obtained from the IMF, Washington, D.C. 20431.

Other international organizations that issue useful economic statistics on a regular basis include the Paris-based Organization for Economic Cooperation and Development and the Brussels-based European Common Market. A major European country that provides an assortment of leading indicators on a regular basis is the United Kingdom. Britain's Central Statistical Office began in 1975 issuing leading indicators in a publication called *Economic Trends* that is similar to *Business Conditions Digest.* In Asia, the Japanese government also provides such data on a regular basis.

Unfortunately, the United Nations is of little use in this regard. It does issues an array of economic statistics for its many members. However, UN economic statistics generally emerge so long after the fact that they are of limited use to anyone trying to keep a tab on unfolding economic developments at home or abroad.

Various private organizations also regularly provide helpful information that bears on international economic developments. Outstanding among these is Morgan Guaranty Trust, whose bimonthly report, World Financial Markets, contains thoughtful analyses on subjects ranging from world stock-market trends to the Third World debt problem.

Altogether, the amount of material on international economic matters that is available from governmental and private sources can easily overwhelm anyone who merely may wish to be reasonably well informed about developments. It is unfortunate that no single source, such as *Business Conditions Digest,* exists in the international area.

Unfortunately as well, the quality of much of the information from abroad remains less reliable than that of most U.S. data. And we have observed that even U.S. statistics are less than perfect.

Still, such statistics do give an idea of important trends that may be under way abroad. The Columbia Center's effort is certainly a move in the right direction. There is little that U.S. officials can do to improve the compilation of statistics, say, in Italy. Many foreign countries, in addition, have suffered far worse inflation than the United States. Inflation, we have seen, can distort economic indicators to a point where they may mislead rather than lead.

Trying to keep abreast of economic developments in the less-developed areas of the globe, or in Communist areas, is hampered to an even greater extent by a scarcity of reliable, comparable data. Until recently, for instance, Brazil's "consumer-price index"—published regularly in such places as the IMF's *International Financial Statistics*—was actually an index only for consumer prices in the city of Rio de Janeiro. To make matters worse, the index did not include housing prices. These had been removed from the index in the late 1960s, at a time when Brazilian officials were under much criticism for failing to bring down the country's high rate of inflation. Housing prices, as it happened, were among the most swiftly rising prices in the index. Their removal, done without publicity, naturally slowed the rise of the index and made Brazil's entire inflation picture appear a good deal brighter than it really was.

Brazilian officials have taken steps to improve the accuracy of their economic statistics, including their price gauges. However, many other less-developed countries, without Brazil's resources, still issue crude, unreliable data that should be treated with much skepticism but is carried in IMF publications and elsewhere.

Such data should nonetheless not be discarded out of hand. The economic importance of such countries is bound to increase further in coming years. As economic information about the world around us continues to improve, our understanding of the U.S. economy, as well as of other economies, should inevitably grow. As Brazil has recently attempted to improve its statistics, so other countries will surely also begin to provide more and better economic information about themselves. This, of course, is all to the good. For on the economic front, as on other fronts, we can no longer afford simply to survey the U.S. scene by itself. A broader view is required.

CHAPTER 10

THE ECONOMY YOU CAN'T SEE

Until now, we have focused in the main on the economy as it appears through many statistical barometers—some good and some not so good, some of long standing and some of relatively recent vintage—that analysts in and out of Washington have devised to help us keep abreast of the broad business scene. For all the progress that has been made in this regard, however, it must be noted that a vast slice of economic activity, abroad as well as at home, largely defies precise description.

This is what analysts call the underground economy. By definition, it is that fraction of overall activity—the exact percentage remains unknown—that is carried on off the books and out of the tax collector's view. Such transactions may range from illicit income derived through assorted criminal activities to the cash you happily pay the neighborhood plumber for fixing that leak in the kitchen that would cost you 30 percent more if you paid the bill by check.

James J. O'Leary, an economic consultant to United States Trust Company in New York, aptly defines the underground economy as "that in which payments are generally made in cash or through barter arrangements so that they are not included in official personal income statistics and are not reported for personal income tax purposes." He goes on to cite "avoidance of personal income tax payments as the underlying motive" for the underground economy, which, he reckons, has increased mightily—though no one knows by just how much—over the post–World War II era.

Though the underground economy can't be gauged with the same degree of precision as its above-ground counterpart, it should not be disregarded in any effort to attain a rounded sense of the general economic picture. It may not be a part of the gross national product, which we have carefully considered earlier, but it nonetheless exerts an important force on overall economic activity in ways that are subtle and not widely recognized.

To understand this influence, an effort first must be made, however imprecise, to illustrate the magnitude and growth of these subterranean transactions. There are no certain figures, quite obviously, but various analysts at various times have conducted noble attempts to pin things down at least a little. The techniques used, like the findings that emerge, differ one from another by considerable amounts. Some researchers, for instance, have focused on the growth of currency within the sundry money-supply components, described earlier, and have deduced from what they deem to be its overly rapid expansion, in terms of total economic activity, that cash transactions, conducted off the books, have assumed a progressively larger role on the business scene as the postwar decades have unfolded. Other researchers have tackled the task through other approaches, which often have involved esoteric statistical techniques of little concern here. What is important, however, is the widespread conclusion, no matter what the avenue of research, that the underground economy has reached enormous proportions and deserves our careful attention.

The range of estimates of size is wide indeed, reaching as high as nearly one third of all business transactions in the United States, according to a study by Edgar L. Fiege, an economist at the University of Wisconsin. On the low end of scale is an analysis published in April 1986 by the Union Bank of Switzerland, which puts the rate at close to 10 percent of America's gross national product. Even that relatively low percentage, of course, works out to hundreds of billions of dollars. The bank's report, it should be added, shows that in many other countries a far higher percentage of overall activity is carried on underground, and that the percentages have been rising rapidly. A few examples: In Sweden, 13.2 percent of GNP, up from 5.4 percent in 1960; in Belgium, 12.1 percent, up from 4.7 percent; in Denmark, 11.8 percent, up from 3.7 percent; in Italy, 11.4 percent, up from 4.4 percent. Still other studies show not only higher rates of underground activity abroad, but even faster growth. By some estimates, for example, Italy's underground economy now accounts for close to 40 percent of overall business dealings there.

A reasonably typical assessment of the U.S. situation, between extremes, has been made by Mr. O'Leary of U.S. Trust. By his reckoning, "the underground economy has become very large and has grown at a very high rate," especially in the period from 1970 to 1985. In that year, he estimates, some $432 billion in off-the-books income coursed through the U.S. economy. This was down somewhat from his estimate for 1984 of $558 billion but dwarfed the comparable totals for most earlier years—for example, $6.6 billion in 1978 and only $4 billion in 1971. The 1984 figure, a record, amounted to as much as 21 percent of personal income, as officially compiled and reported by Washington's statistics mills. Even with the year-to-year drop, the 1985 underground total came to more than 15 percent of that year's official income figure.

Carol Carson, an economist at the Commerce Department who has done extensive research into the size and makeup of the underground economy, has compiled a list of the sorts of activities that underlie its enormous income flow. These components include many, if not most, "moonlighting" jobs that countless people take on to supplement earnings from their primary employment, enterprises such as smuggling; gambling and prostitution, where they are outlawed; working without a necessary permit, as do many illegal aliens; illegal trade in drugs; padding expense accounts; working for unreported tips; theft; and covert home rentals. This last activity is greater than one might suppose. George Sternlieb, director of the Center for Urban Policy Research at Rutgers University, has estimated that there are some 2,000,000 within-the-house "apartments" in the United States, and that at least half of these units belong to owners who have surreptitiously constructed them—for example, in basements and attics—and collect on the average $3,000 per year per unit in rent that is not reported as income.

Another huge source of underground income, other studies show, is income generated by Americans living abroad. A Congressional study finds that in 1985, for example, U.S. citizens residing in foreign areas evaded paying as much as $2 billion in federal taxes that they owed in the United States. While only about 5 percent of Americans living in the United States failed to file returns that year, the study shows that the Internal Revenue Service received only 2,012 returns from 55,000 Americans living in Brazil, only 3,831 returns from 90,000 citizens residing in Italy and only 2,186 returns from 40,800 Americans living in Greece.

Such reports are obviously disturbing on account of the attitudes they reveal. Among other things, laws are clearly being broken, and there is the important matter of fairness. But there also is a much larger reason for concern about such activities, for they contribute, along with all the other sorts of subterranean endeavor, to a situation—the thriving underground economy—that renders economic policy-making less effective and, ultimately, works against the economy's general good health.

Consider, for example, the matter of the perennial deficits in the federal budget, no small worry in the decade of the 1980s. If off-the-books income had been properly taxed through the period, the level of budgetary red ink would have been far lower or, by some estimates, would have disappeared altogether. This, in turn, would have served to ease credit-market pressures and thus reduce interest-rate levels, since the government's borrowing needs would have been far less. It follows that, in such circumstances, the economy would most likely have shown more vigorous growth than was the case.

Economic policymakers, of course, depend in their decisions in large measure on the numbers that the country's statisticians manage to produce each day or week or month or quarter. But the underground economy leaves a very big blank spot on the radar screen. And this can lead to major policy mistakes. If the Labor Department's official numbers show a worrisome rise in the jobless rate, for instance, policymakers may opt to stimulate business activity, perhaps through an easier monetary policy at the Federal Reserve or perhaps through a mix of stimulative moves on the fiscal front. Such tactics may be fine if joblessness is indeed on the rise, as the official numbers indicate. But if the decline in reported jobs is being offset, or more than offset, by increasing employment in the underground economy, then such maneuvers could prove inflationary, stimulating an economy that is running much closer to full capacity than is supposed.

On a happier note, many analysts estimate, on account of the underground economy, that American may be a good deal less spendthrift than official figures suggest. Commerce Department data show, for instance, that in 1969 personal savings amounted to 6.4 percent of after-tax income, while the comparable reading in 1981 was only 5.3 percent, and the rate continued to decline in subsequent years. But a very different picture emerges if one uses other data, taken from Federal Reserve reports of monetary inflows to financial institutions, as well as from Fed estimates of cash held by households. By this calculation, the 1969 saving rate of 6.4 percent rises modestly to 6.5 percent and the 1981 rate of 5.3 percent jumps to 9.6 percent. Through this 12-year period, of course, inflation was pushing people into higher and higher tax brackets, creating a rising pressure to supplement above-ground income with underground dollars. Reviewing the saving-rate surge, at least in unofficial terms, Otto Eckstein of Data Resources remarked that the rate based on the Fed data was no doubt "more reliable" than the Commerce data. He went on to conclude that "the depressed official saving rate is probably a statistical illusion." By measuring money flowing into financial institutions, he explained, the Federal Reserve data pick up vast sums of "underground income" that the Commerce data, which depend on reported wage and other income, largely fail to embrace.

In the wake of the 1981 to 1982 recession, of course, inflation eased markedly in the United States. Moreover, Congress enacted legislation aimed at preventing inflationary "bracket creep" in the tax rates people must pay. In addition, repeated cuts in the top personal income-tax rates constituted a key part of President Reagan's economic program, and he was able to win congressional approval for the reductions.

Such developments would seem likely to arrest or even reverse the growth of the underground economy, just as rising inflation and taxes surely spurred its rise in earlier decades. And there is some evidence that this has happened. The numbers compiled by Mr. O'Leary of United States Trust, as noted earlier,

show a decline in the underground income flow in 1985 of some
$126 billion—no minor sum. Other research, conducted by the
New York investment firm of Sanford C. Bernstein & Company,
shows a similar recent shrinkage and attributes the decline
largely to the fact that other data indicate a marked reduction
in the share of American job holders who are self-employed. It
has fallen, according to the report, from about one fifth in the
early postwar years to about one tenth in recent years. Hiding
income, the study argues, is far more difficult when one works
for, say, a large corporation than for one's self.

At the same time, various government efforts—some more
successful than others—have been launched to unearth underground activity. The campaign, moreover, is by no means limited
to the federal government. Consider, for instance, steps taken in
New York City. By estimates of the Internal Revenue Service,
fully 20 percent of the city's business activity has been conducted
underground in recent years. This would come to roughly $40
billion annually, based on the size of the city's economy in the
late 1980s. In terms of missed revenues for the city—unpaid
sales, property, and income taxes—some $1 billion has been lost
each year to its underground economy.

Under its finance commissioner, Abraham Biderman, however, the city in 1987 initiated a concerted drive to curb off-the-
books activity and capture lost revenue. It boosted its staff of
auditors, investigators, and back-office personnel to over 1,000.
As a result of the beefed-up force, the city agents have been able
to look more closely at a variety of suspicious matters—for instance, a return that shows a $50,000 car or a $500,000 condom-
inium apartment purchased by a taxpayer showing income of,
say, $30,000.

In addition, a little-noted provision of the Tax Reform Act of
1986 permits cities like New York to tap more fully information
in the hands of the Internal Revenue Service. New York officials
have begun to make use of this. Another tactic has been simply,
with the increased staff of investigators, to observe particular
businesses more closely. "Our auditors might go to a restaurant
and have lunch," Mr. Biderman explained in a 1987 interview
with the New York Daily News. "They observe the guy serving

200 to 300 lunches a day, and his receipts are only 100 a day. We recently had an instance where auditors found the owner sitting in front of his restaurant shooing people away, because he knew auditors were there. He understood on that day he didn't want to have successful business."

The 1986 tax legislation also, of course, cut the top income-tax rates sharply, which presumably would tend to bring underground activity out into the open, just as higher taxes tended earlier to force more transactions below ground. Early signs, however, have suggested that once business has been carried on underground, bringing it back into the open is no easy task, whatever may be happening to taxes. Tax-cutting obviously "lowers the value of cheating relative to the penalty," notes William Dunkelberg, a Temple University dean and economics professor. However, in early 1988, Byron L. Dorgan, a former state tax commissioner who led a 1987 government task force on tax problems stemming from the underground economy, told the New York Times that "I don't know of any evidence that it has shrunk." And Donald H. Skadden, an officer of the American Institute of Certified Public Accountants, suggests that many Americans have come to view tax cheating as a way of life. "Once people learned how to evade 70 percent taxes, they would continue to evade" taxes at lower and lower rates, he says.

Another factor, according to Phillip L. Mann, a Washington lawyer specializing in tax matters, may be the natural hesitancy of anyone to report suddenly a very sharp increase in income. This, he says, could prompt revenue agents to ask such questions as, "How come your income went up so much this year?" Still another factor, some analysts say, is that while federal income-tax rates indeed did fall during the Reagan presidential years, the state and local tax burden has generally risen, largely offsetting any relief from federal rate cutting. All the while, moreover, the Social Security tax burden has risen apace.

An American Bar Association group that looked into the tax compliance problem in mid-1987 concluded, rather gloomily, that the share of taxes that Americans pay voluntarily "is probably about the same" as just before federal income-tax rates began to fall early in the decade. M. Bernard Aidinoff, who headed the panel, remarked that he very much doubted, in fact, that tax "rates have very much to do with" the persistence of the underground economy, now that it has become so well established.

The prospect that the underground economy, like death and taxes, will always be with us is disheartening, to be sure—at least for those of us who do pay the tax collector what's due. Quite apart from such considerations, however, an appreciation of the magnitude of off-the-books transactions helps us all—whatever taxes we do or do not pay—to understand a little better the full dimensions of an economy that deserves a good deal more attention than it often gets.

INDEX

A

Ackley, Gardner, 102–103
A.F.L.-C.I.O., 13, 17
Aidinoff, M. Bernard, 164
Allan, John, 137
Argus Research Corporation, 121–122
Automobile sales, as economic indicator, 99–101

B

Balance of payments
  international, 47–49
    and balance of trade, 48–49
    deficits, 48
    scope of statement, 47–48
    surpluses, 48
Balance of trade
  in GNP, 19–20
  and international balance of payments, 48–49
  trade figures, 48–49
Bank Credit Analyst, 70–71
Biderman, Abraham, 163
Bienstock, Herbert, 39, 41
Boston Company, The, 45
Bracket creep, 162
Bretton Woods, 148–149
Budget deficits, 115–116
  cause of, 115

Bureau of Labor Statistics, 12
  consumer-price index (CPI), 23–29
  monthly report, contents of, 12
  producer-price index, 28–30
  productivity estimates, 40–41, 50–51
  standard of living measure, 32–35
  unemployment rate, 12–17
    calculation of, 15–17
    monthly report, 12–13
Burns, Arthur F., 57, 89, 105
Business Conditions Digest
  economic forecasting, 102–103, 125–130
  international economic activity, 154–155
Business cycles. *See* Economic cycles
Business planning, and economic cycles, 62–64

C

Capacity utilization rate, 43–44
Capitalism, and economic stability, 93
Carson, Carol, 160
Carter, Jimmy, 8
Census Bureau, 15, 16
Center for International Business Cycle Research, 154
Central Statistical Office, Great Britain, 155
Cohen, Morris, 61